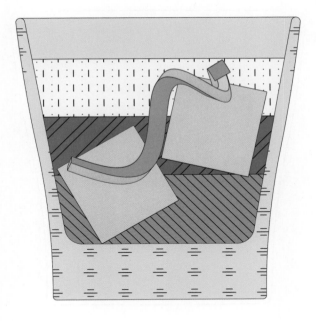

THE
ULTIMATE
BOOK OF
COCKTAILS

Published in 2020 by Hardie Grant Books, an imprint of Hardie Grant Publishing

Hardie Grant Books (London)
5th & 6th Floors
52–54 Southwark Street
London SE1 1UN

Hardie Grant Books (Melbourne)
Building 1, 658 Church Street
Richmond, Victoria 3121

hardiegrantbooks.com

British Library Cataloguing-in-Publication Data. A catalogue record for this book is available from the British Library.

The Ultimate Book of Cocktails
ISBN: 978-1-78488-347-8

10 9 8 7 6 5

Publishing Director: Kate Pollard
Editor: Eila Purvis
Art Direction: Matt Phare
Illustrator: Daniel Servansky
Indexer: Cathy Heath

Colour Reproduction by p2d
Printed and bound in China by Leo Paper Products Ltd.

THE
ULTIMATE
BOOK OF
COCKTAILS

Dan Jones

Illustrations by Daniel Servansky

Hardie Grant

BOOKS

CONTENTS

Welcome to

THE

ULTIMATE

BOOK OF

COCKTAILS

WELL, HELLO

'WE ARE ALL IN THE GUTTER, BUT SOME OF US ARE LOOKING AT THE STARS.'

– Oscar Wilde, *Lady Windermere's Fan*, Act III

Does anything describe sweet inebriation by the world's finest booze better than Oscar Wilde's infamous quote? That tickle of fizz, the sharp slap of citrus, the aroma of fresh botanicals and the intimate massage of perfectly refined, potent alcohol that leaves many of us rolling around in the gutter: cocktails build you up, knock you down, and encourage the sending of inappropriate selfies to everyone in your contacts.

Perhaps Wilde didn't quite mean booze when he came up with that legendary line (although he was, apparently, an absinthe man), but his knowledge of alcohol and its otherworldly effects is undeniable. And what a story each spirit has! Take gin, for instance: from its troubled birth on the backstreets of London

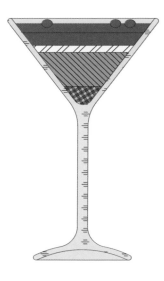

potion administered to break fevers, clean wounds, warm your chilliest bits and mend broken hearts; its power was immense. Eastern Europe was in thrall to the clear, powerful spirit (much like England's cross-eyed love affair with gin) and it very nearly brought Russia to its knees when workers were struck with rising bar debts and horrible hangovers.

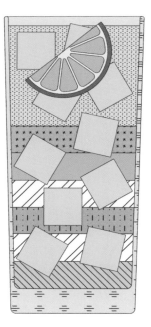

to its current incarnation as the world's fastest-growing artisanal spirit, gin's salacious past and rosy future is as tasty as a freshly made G & T. Then, there's rum. The drink that powered hoary old sea-farers across the oceans in search of new worlds, or marauders in search of mythical treasure; kick-starting rebellions and *coups d'état*, and fuelling countless gals' party nights (what was that stripper's name, again?).

And what about vodka? In ages past, it was a mysterious cure-all, a magic

Tequila tastes of Guadalajaran skies, desert heat and verdant blue-green leaves, distilled down via an ancient recipe into a crystal-clear, power-punch of a spirit. The roots of our most beloved, hangover-inducing spirit go all the way back to the Aztecs, almost 2,000 years ago.

And whisky, the amber spirit aged in wooden casks. Loved (and made) all around the world, from peppery rye to blended bourbon, soft and sweet.

This is *The Ultimate Book of Cocktails* – a full cocktail list of classic recipes, tropical wonders and dinner party crowd-pleasers; contemporary concoctions, interesting twists on old faithfuls, and the perfect Bloody Mary. Plus, homemade syrups and sours, retro greatest hits, and mouth-watering new uses for cucumbers.

A perfectly mixed cocktail – lively with citrus, or chilled to frosty perfection – delivered at just the right time, in just the right glass, truly takes the edge off. It can underline the mood, smooth things out or pep them up.

There's an art to it; here's how to mix it, shake it, stir it and drink it: all-in-one to get things done. Now, let's have a drink.

Dan Jones

The World's Best Spirits

Tried and tested: from the finest premium brands
for perfect mixing to single-estate sippers and
sassy little flavoured numbers, from all four corners
of the globe.

BEST RUM FOR TIME TRAVELLERS

DARK MATTER SPICED RUM

To Scotland, where the mysterious award-winning Dark Matter distillery weaves its magic in liquid form. They describe their blended rum as, 'The taste equivalent of warping into a liquid black hole…' with fiery fresh ginger, green peppercorns and allspice.

BEST RUM FOR SMOOTH OPERATORS

HAVANA CLUB 7

Smooth and creamy, this is the original contemporary rum. Havana Club is the ultimate rum brand (and should be your first port of call when schooling yourself in this magical spirit); founded in Cuba in 1934.

BEST RUM FOR BOURBON LOVERS

EAST LONDON LIQUOR DEMERARA RUM

This craft distiller, based in an old glue factory in east London, uses uses 100 per cent demerara sugar molasses from Guyana and distills in the world's only surviving wooden column still, and then ages in bourbon barrels for three years.

BEST VODKA FOR LEATHER-LOVERS

TOM OF FINLAND VODKA

A refined, organic wheat and rye spirit blended with Arctic spring water celebrates the life and art of Touko Laaksonen, AKA Tom of Finland. Smooth as a leather jock strap.

BEST VODKA FOR WANNABE ROYALS

ZUBROWKA

Zubrowka is the king of Polish vodkas, which is flavoured with a special kind of aromatic bison grass grown wild in the heart of Bialowieza Forest and harvested by hand.

BEST VODKA FOR SHEEP-LOVERS

HARTSHORN DISTILLERY SHEEP WHEY

Young Tasmanian devil Ryan Hartshorn's Sheep Whey Vodka uses a by-product from his family's cheese business to create a caramel, fruity vodka that won Best Vodka at the World Vodka Awards 2018.

BEST GIN FOR DRUNKEN KOALA LOVERS

FOUR PILLARS

To Australia and the picturesque Yarra Valley in Victoria, where the tiny Four Pillars distillery creates its excellent barrel-aged gin using triple-filtered water and a curious recipe of botanicals – local, exotic and traditional.

BEST GIN FOR OFFBEAT ODDBALLS

CONKER SPIRIT DORSET DRY

Like it smooth? Rupert Holloway sure does. The Dorset-based gin-maker has created what is perhaps the UK's smoothest, softest, and most off-beat gin, the Dorset Dry.

BEST GIN FOR NATURAL BUSH-LOVERS

ARCHIE ROSE GIN

Sydney's Archie Rose Distillery's Signature Dry Gin uses native Australian botanicals like blood lime, lemon myrtle and river mint. Delicious.

BEST TEQUILA FOR CELEB SIPPERS

CASAMIGOS AÑEJO TEQUILA

With smoldering silver fox George Clooney as co-owner, Casamigos has something of an unfair advantage; but it's a spicy little number with a soft vanilla tone and fresh mint finish.

BEST TEQUILA FOR TEQUILA GEEKS

TAPATIO BLANCO TEQUILA

Tapatio tequila gives the bar trade fizzy knickers: it's the cult brand that has a smooth, premium taste at an old school price. A great starter-tequila for the home-cocktail maker.

BEST TEQUILA FOR TRADITIONALISTS

QUIQUIRIQUI MEZCAL

This small-batch brand of single-estate Mezcals boasts zero industrial jiggery pokery in favour of age-old growing, harvesting, squishing and pit-roasting techniques.

BEST WHISKEY FOR SMOKY SPIRITUALISTS

BUFFALO TRACE KENTUCKY BOURBON

This award-winning, 220+ year-old distillery's Kentucky bourbon has aromas of vanilla, mint and molasses with a smooth mouthfeel. Perfect for the bourbon novice.

BEST WHISKY FOR BUFFALO BROS

LAPHROAIG

This peaty scotch from the Islay region of Scotland is a solid, 10-year-old spirit with seaweed, vanilla and smoke flavours. Great for breaking yourself into smoky spirits.

BEST WHISKEY FOR HIGH SOCIETY TYPES

HUDSON MANHATTAN RYE

Made from wholegrain rye, this is a classic, spicy, rustic rye whiskey with surprising smoothness. A great sipper with a herby edge.

Essential Gadgetry

Build up your home bar with a few minimal essentials to make the world's most marvellous margaritas, punches, martinis and sours.

IMPRESSIVE TOOLS

Create your own at-home bar with a range of nifty cocktail-making tools. Start off simple: a shaker, jigger, strainer and an ice bucket. Here's what you'll need to keep it minimal:

JIGGER

A toolbox essential. The jigger is the standard measure for spirits and liqueurs, and is available in many different sizes. Heavy metallic jiggers look the part, but plastic or glass versions also do the job. If you don't have a jigger or single-shot glass, use an egg cup as a stand-in – at least then your ratios will be right, even if your shots might be a little generous – failing that, cross your fingers and free-pour your drinks.

2oz (60ml)

1.5oz (44ml)

SAUCER

Some bartenders use a 'rimming dish' to add the salt or sugar rim to a glass. If you think, like me, that just sounds weird, just use a saucer with a larger diameter than the glass.

SHAKER

Sometimes known as the Boston shaker, it's the home mixer's silver bullet. This is your single most important piece of kit as very few cocktails are possible without one. The classic metallic model has three main parts: a base, known as the 'can' (a tall, tumbler shape that tapers out), a tight-fitting funnel top with built-in strainer, onto which a small cap fits (which can also be used as a jigger). It's brilliantly straightforward and, like all fine tools, it pays to keep it scrupulously clean. If you can't get your hands on one, consider a large glass jar with a lid and waterproof seal.

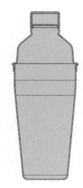

MIXING GLASS

A simple, sturdy, straight-sided glass (also known as 'the Boston') – or a straight-sided pint glass that tapers out – are great for cocktails that need stirring with a bar spoon rather than shaking. To allow for extra volume when attached to the can of your shaker (to make two or more drinks at a time), the two halves are locked together and shaken until the drink is chilled, then a Hawthorne strainer can be used to strain the drink into a glass.

HAWTHORNE STRAINER

This showy-looking strainer, trimmed with a spring, comes in handy when your shaker's built-in version isn't up to the job. Place on a glass and pour the cocktail through it, or hold up against the cocktail can or mixing glass and pour from a height. Wash immediately after use. A fine tea strainer does the job brilliantly, but the classic Hawthorne looks the part.

BLENDER

Essential for fruity little numbers. Unless you're using a NutriBullet, most domestic blenders find ice a challenge, so it's best to use crushed ice in blended cocktails. Add your ingredients first, then the ice, and start off on a slow speed before turning it up to max. No need to strain. Once the consistency is super smooth, pour into a glass and serve.

CHOPPING BOARD AND KNIFE

Simple, but essential. Keep the board clean, the knife super sharp and practise your peeling skills: the aim is to avoid as much white pith as possible, leaving just the zest that is studded with aromatic oils.

ICE BUCKET

The centrepiece of your home bar. It can be simple, functional and slightly retro, or the full plastic pineapple. An insulated ice bucket means your ice cubes will keep their shape for longer, and a good set of vintage tongs adds a touch of class.

UPSCALE EXTRAS

ICE PICK

Buy bags of filtered crushed ice or cubes (and always buy double or triple the amount you think you'll need), or attack your own homemade ice block with an ice pick. Boil water, let it cool slightly and pour into an old plastic ice-cream container. Freeze solid, turn out onto a clean tea (dish) towel, and then attack as needed – keeping a firm grip. The ice will go everywhere, but bear with it. Keep the shards large and jagged.

MUDDLER

A short, usually wooden baton used to mash and muddle fruit, herbs, ice and sugar in the glass. Bruising and bashing up the ingredients releases their natural oils and flavours. Think of it as a pestle for your drink. If you don't have a muddler, use a flat-ended rolling pin.

NOVELTY STRAWS, PARASOLS AND PLASTIC MONKEYS

Tricky. Creating hands-down amazing cocktails means that they should taste and look incredible just as they are. That's without parasols, plastic monkeys, flashing LED ice cubes and novelty straws you can also wear as glasses. That said, there's something more than a little pleasing about adding the odd frill to your drink. Make sure paper straws are part of your home bar toolkit – stripy red and white ones are pretty eye-catching – and the odd plastic monkey never hurt anyone. Maybe save your penis straws for extra-special occasions like 80th birthday parties or funerals – things like that.

CITRUS PRESS

Always, always, always use fresher-than-fresh citrus juices. Never skimp on this part of drink-making. If you don't have a citrus press or squeezer, use your hands. Roll and squish your fruit on a hard surface to loosen it up, slice in half, then squeeze through your fingers, catching the pips as you go.

BAR SPOON

The classic bar spoon has a long, twisted (or sometimes flat) handle, a flat end and a teardrop-shaped spoon used for stirring and measuring out ingredients. It's not essential, but it looks pretty cool.

CANELE OR JULIENNE KNIFE

A fancy bit of kit: the canele knife has a V-shaped groove for cutting citrus peel spirals, carving melons and probably many other crafty uses. Not essential, but great to have.

COCKTAIL STICK

For spearing cherries, citrus peel, fruit slices, olives, onion slivers, pickles, sausages, cleaning under your nails, etc.

SWIZZLE STICK

More than just cocktail furniture, the swizzle allows the drinker to navigate their own drink, stirring as they go. Great for drinks packed with fruit or garnishes, or for nervous partygoers who need something to fiddle with.

A Guide to Glasses

You can serve a delicious cocktail in just about anything:
a chipped coffee mug, Dora the Explorer party cups, a
shoe, but it's best to invest in the proper glassware — and
keep each one squeaky clean.

COUPE

The short, trumpet-shaped glass perfect for Champagne and sparkling wines and a respectable Martini glass alternative. Invest in a vintage set – it's worth it.

MARTINI

Cocktail culture's most iconic glass: the refined stem and cone-shaped glass flares out to create a large, shallow recess. Somehow it loses its ability not to slosh out its contents as the evening wears on. (**Fig. 1**)

FIG. 2

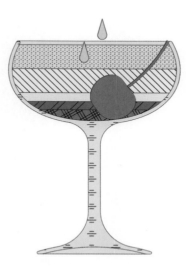

FIG. 1

MARGARITA

There's no other way to drink a Margie than from its official wide glass; it's the wonky, one-toothed cousin of the Martini glass, with a bulbous bottom and a yearning to meet the lips of a handsome stranger. (**Fig. 2**)

JULEP CUP

The little, stainless steel or copper cup that frosts in seconds and fits neatly inside most shakers. A hangover from 1800s Kentucky cocktail culture.

BOSTON GLASS

The twin brother of the straight-sided pint glass, swapped at birth. Great for mixing in or for using locked into the can of your shaker.

SHOT GLASS

Short and simple. Pour, drink, slam down. Done. Also doubles as a jigger.

HIGHBALL

Ostensibly a tall glass with a thick and sturdy bottom that holds 225–350 ml (8–12 oz) of perfectly mixed booze. (**Fig. 3**)

TUMBLER

The short glass that's perfect for short or single-shot drinks. Like most things, best to pick one with a heavy bottom. (**Fig. 4**)

LARGE WINE GLASS

The one your Auntie Sharon drinks her chardonnay from and then demands to speak to the manager. (**Fig. 5**)

FIG. 3

FIG. 5

FIG. 4

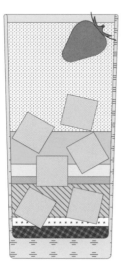

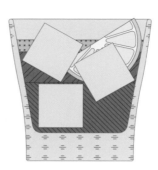

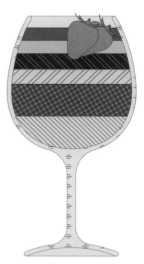

TIKI GLASS

The tiki glass was born in mid-20th-century American tiki bars and attributed to Don the Beachcomber, the founding father of tiki culture. It's a tall, wonky-looking glass with a face like an Easter Island statue. (**Fig. 6**)

JAM JAR

There are no hard-and-fast rules for how to serve your drinks – or rather what you serve them in. You can use any number of alternatives – jam jars, tea cups, sciencey test tubes and beakers, Russian tea glasses, and shoes – to get your guests beyond the pale. (**Fig. 7**)

COLLINS GLASS

The skinny, usually straight-sided version of the highball. (**Fig. 8**)

PUNCH GLASS

Ornate, sometimes with handles, and small-ish so your guests don't get too tipsy too quickly.

FIG. 6

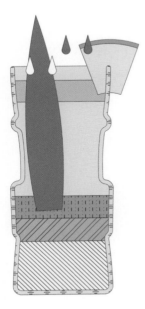

FIG. 7

FIG. 8

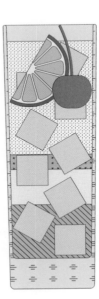

Tricks of the Trade

It's not just the quality of your tool, it's how you use it.
How to shake, muddle, stir, and mix it all up.

HOW TO DO IT

HOW TO SHAKE

There's a war going on in cocktail land. How long to shake to get the perfect concoction? No one can agree. Some say 15 seconds of brisk shaking, others say less. This book is going out on a limb and settling on a short and sharp seven seconds. Any longer could dilute the drink a little too much, affecting potency. There should be no bottle-flipping or sparkler-lighting, although a little lemon-and-lime juggling wouldn't go amiss.

HOW TO STIR

Whip out your bar spoon and your mixing glass, and stir gently and deftly with ice to chill the concoction. When condensation forms on the outside of the glass, it's ready to go.

HOW TO CHILL

If you have room, clear a shelf in your freezer and keep your cocktail glasses on ice, or pack them full of cubes and then discard when the glass is chilled.

POTENCY

All cocktails are potent, but some are more potent than others. Each drink should seek to achieve a perfect balance of flavours and can attempt differing levels of intensity, but shouldn't get you drunk – at least

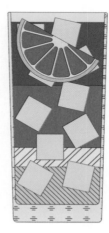

not on its own. Perfect measurements really matter.

THE LOOK

Fresh garnishes, squeaky clean glasses, clear, purified ice and a perfect balance of colours and visible textures are essential.

AROMATICS

Your drink should not just taste good – it should smell really, really great. Bitters, fresh juices and citrus peels packed with fragrant oils help achieve this.

THE BACK BAR

Create a back bar with a mix of strong, clean and classic spirits, adding in your own infusions and oddities in your own sweet time. Reserve your finest, aged and premium spirits for simple concoctions (quality can sometimes be obscured in the mixing of particularly complex, fruity numbers) and sippers, and have some medium-range pourers on hand. Start with some craft gin, light and dark rum, whisky or bourbon, depending on your preference, a premium vodka and delicious tequila, plus white and red vermouth, and an amaro or apertif liqueur. Throw in your favourite bitters, a vegan foamer like Ms Better's Miraculous Foamer Bitters, and you're all set.

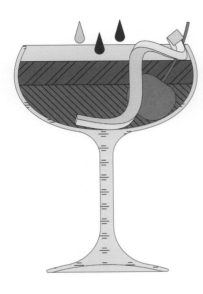

SYRUP

Essential. Simple syrup – AKA
gomme or sugar syrup – is liquid
sugar and, mixed part-for-part
with sharp citrus juices, brings
a delightfully sweet-sour note to
a drink. Buy a premium version
of simple syrup (Monin is a
decent brand) or make your
own (page 29).

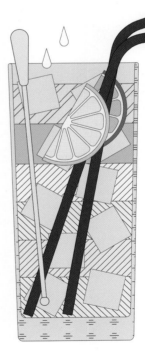

BITTERS

Said to be a cure for hiccups,
Angostura (the Venezuelan-by-way-
of-Trinidad-and-Tobago) bitters are
an essential element of the back bar.
The part-herbal, part-alcoholic
tincture is highly aromatic, giving
cocktails a depth and complexity of
flavour, and colouring white spirits
a subtle, sunrise pink. Bitters and
cordial producers Fee Brothers
(est. 1863) is another good brand
to start with: their rhubarb and
plum and whisky barrel-aged bitters
are particularly mouth-caving.

Syrups, Sours & More

Create your own delicious infused booze,
the perfect cocktail syrups, flavoured syrups
and sour mixes.

Simple Syrup

INGREDIENTS
200 ml (7 oz) water
100 g (3½ oz) demerara, cane
    or granulated sugar
1 tbsp golden syup or corn
    syrup (optional)

EQUIPMENT
Non-stick saucepan, wooden
spoon, funnel

GLASS
200 ml (7 oz) sterilised Kilner
(Mason) jar or glass bottle
with stopper

METHOD
Boil the water in the saucepan
and gently add the sugar. Turn
down the heat and stir
constantly with a wooden
spoon for 3–5 minutes until all
the sugar is dissolved and the
syrup is clear. Turn off the heat
and leave to cool. While still
runny, pour into a sterilised
Kilner jar or pour through a
funnel into a sterilised glass
bottle with stopper. Adding a
spoonful of golden syrup to the
cooled mixture will help keep
it smooth. Store in the fridge
for up to six weeks.

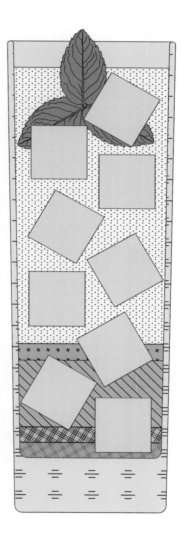

Coffee Power

Perfect for coffee geeks who love to booze: a vanilla-powered infusion that's simple to make and even easier to drink. Slip a shot of this in your travel mug.

INGREDIENTS

1 split vanilla pod (bean)
600 ml (20 oz) blanco tequila
100 g (31/2 oz) freshly ground coffee
100 ml (31/2 oz) Demerara Simple
　　　Syrup (see flavoured syrup
　　　method, page 31)

METHOD

Add a vanilla pod to your tequila and leave to infuse for 24–72 hours (check daily as you want a gentle vanilla taste;

Sweet & Sour Mix

Sweet & Sour is the name given to the perfect balance of sugar syrup and fresh citrus juice that can be made ahead of time (it's equal parts simple syrup and citrus juice) or created in small amounts per drink.

if you leave it too long it becomes too floral). When your vanilla infusion is ready, remove the vanilla pod, then add the ground coffee and give it a good shake. Place the tequila in the freezer for at least 72 hours. Strain through a coffee filter, then add a little of the simple syrup, to taste. Shake well.

TIP
Best served in an Espresso Martini or straight from the freezer over ice as a sipping drink.

Flavoured Syrup

INGREDIENTS
200 ml (7 oz) water
100 g (3 oz) demerara, cane
    or granulated sugar
1 tbsp golden syrup or corn
    syrup (optional)

Choose your own flavourings: a thumb-sized piece of fresh, peeled ginger, mashed; rhubarb and star anise; a vanilla pod; basil.

EQUIPMENT
Non-stick saucepan, wooden spoon, funnel

GLASS
200 ml (7 oz) sterilised Kilner (Mason) jar or glass bottle with stopper

METHOD
Boil the water in the saucepan and gently add the sugar and your

flavouring of choice. Turn down the heat and stir constantly with a wooden spoon for 3–5 minutes until all the sugar is dissolved and the syrup is clear. Turn off the heat and leave to cool slightly. Strain through a fine mesh sieve or muslin and then pour into a sterilised Kilner jar or pour through a funnel into a sterilised glass bottle with stopper. Adding a spoonful of golden syrup to the cooled mixture will help keep it smooth. Store in the fridge for up to six weeks.

THE RECIPES

Learn to make members' club classics and their modern reinventions, delicious citrus pick-me-ups, seasonal showstoppers, and more; plus mouth-cavers, butt-tinglers, and the world's most drinkable drinks. Each recipe serves one, unless stated otherwise. Happy drinking.

The Classics

Age-old, classic concoctions top every upscale cocktail list, and so they should. Perfectly balanced, and each with its own secret history, these cocktail recipes hit the spot in the classiest way imaginable.

THE VODKA MARTINI

The ultimate classic cocktail, the Vodka Martini consists of just two ingredients: vodka and vermouth, and is fragranced by a lemon twist. Sometimes stirred in a mixing glass, using the shaker adds a frostiness that numbs any sharpness, making it silky smooth. If someone tells you one can't serve a Martini without gin, cut them out of your life.

INGREDIENTS

1	premium vodka	60 ml (2 oz)
2	dry vermouth	15 ml (½ oz)
3	lemon twist	to garnish

EQUIPMENT

Shaker, strainer

METHOD

Shake the liquids over ice until the shaker is frosty and the liquids are slightly diluted (about 20–30 seconds), then strain into a glass. Garnish with a lemon twist.

GLASS TYPE:
MARTINI OR COUPE

TIP The Martini is only as good as the vodka you use: go premium.

NEGRONI

The tougher, more intense version of the Americano, created in Florence where a hero of the cocktail world thought to replace soda water with gin. What a marvellous man!

INGREDIENTS

1	gin	30 ml (1 oz)
2	sweet vermouth	30 ml (1 oz)
3	Campari	60 ml (2 oz)
4	orange twist	to garnish

EQUIPMENT

Mixing glass, bar spoon

METHOD

Stir the gin, vermouth and Campari in a mixing glass over ice. Strain into a tumbler filled with ice cubes. Garnish with the orange twist.

GLASS TYPE:
TUMBLER

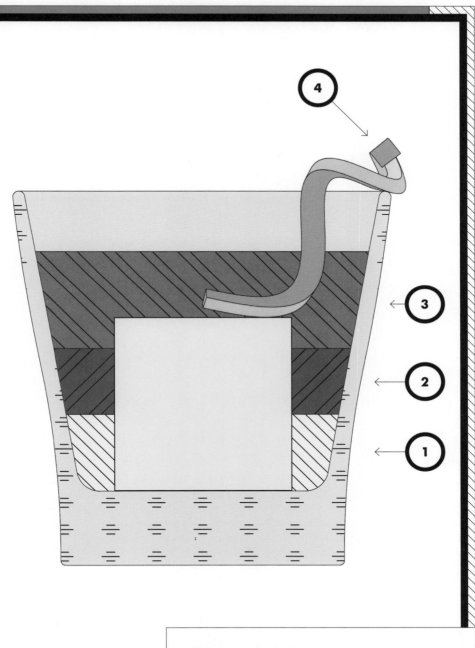

TIP Use a big hunk of ice so it melts slowly (and doesn't dilute your drink before you've finished it).

MOJITO

This legendary Cuban five-way of white rum, sugar, mint, sharp lime and soda water is the island nation's most magical export. Ostensibly a classic Cuban highball, the Mojito's timeless appeal is in its simplicity: although devotees would disagree, it's hard to mess up.

INGREDIENTS

1	lime wedges	2
2	demerara sugar	2 tsp
3	fresh mint leaves	12
4	white rum	60 ml (2 oz)
5	chilled soda water	to top up
6	fresh mint sprig	to garnish

EQUIPMENT

Muddler, bar spoon

METHOD

Muddle the lime wedges and sugar in the highball glass, going hard for more citrus flavour or gentle for a subtler taste. Add the mint leaves and gently muddle. Fill the glass three-quarters full with crushed ice, then add the rum and stir. Finally, add more crushed ice and top with chilled soda water and a mint sprig.

GLASS TYPE:
HIGHBALL

TIP Some say lemonade is a good alternative to soda water: don't even think about it.

COSMOPOLITAN

The taste of the 90s. This pink, sharp, vodka-based cocktail dominated the upscale drinkeries of New York, London and beyond, getting all manner of bright, young bachelorettes tipsy in the process. The Cosmo may have drifted out of the spotlight somewhat, but it's still a classic – and truly delicious.

INGREDIENTS

1	mandarin or premium vodka	50 ml (1¾ oz)
2	triple sec	25 ml (¾ oz)
3	cranberry juice	25 ml (¾ oz)
4	orange twist	to garnish

EQUIPMENT

Shaker, strainer

METHOD

Shake the ingredients with ice and strain into a chilled glass. Garnish with orange twist and serve.

GLASS TYPE:
COUPE OR MARTINI

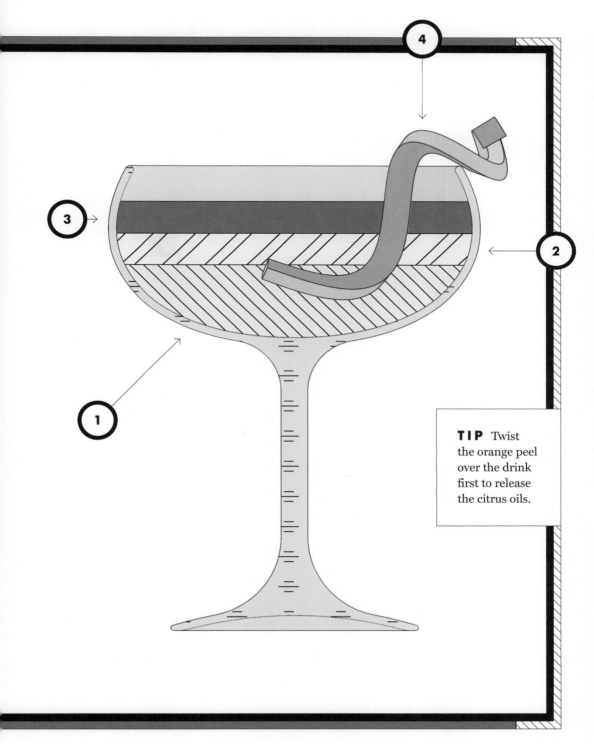

TIP Twist the orange peel over the drink first to release the citrus oils.

ULTIMATE BLOODY MARY

Everyone has their own version of this classic brunch drink, but this garlic, cucumber and horseradish-infused recipe will win anyone over.

INGREDIENTS (SERVES 4)

1	tomato juice	1 litre (34 oz/4 cups)
2	vodka	230 ml (8 oz/1 cup)
3	pickle juice	80 ml (3 oz/⅓ cup)
4	Worcestershire sauce	2 tsp
5	hot creamed horseradish	1 tsp
6	garlic, minced	1 clove
7	cucumber, peeled and seeded	1 medium
8	Tabasco	dash
9	freshly ground black pepper	1 tsp
10	sea salt	generous pinch
11	smoked paprika	1 tsp
12	large pickles, cut into spears	to garnish
13	lemon wedges	to garnish

EQUIPMENT

Blender

METHOD

Blend the ingredients (except from the pickle spears and lemon) then pour into glasses half-filled with ice. Add the pickle spears and lemon to garnish.

GLASS TYPE:
BOSTON
OR HIGHBALL

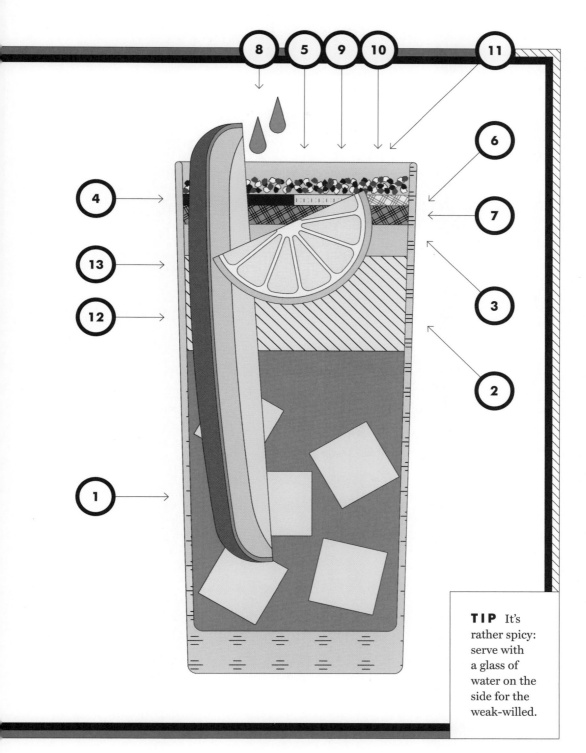

TIP It's rather spicy: serve with a glass of water on the side for the weak-willed.

MOSCOW MULE

The classic vodka cocktail, popular in NYC in the 1940s (and said to be the result of a thrifty bartender's excess stock clear-out), remains one of the finest ways to drink vodka.

INGREDIENTS

1	premium vodka	60 ml (2 oz)
2	lime juice, freshly squeezed	½ lime
3	agave or Simple Syrup (page 29)	30 ml (1 oz)
4	fiery ginger beer	to top up

EQUIPMENT

Shaker, strainer

METHOD

Shake the vodka, lime and syrup with ice, strain into a chilled Moscow mule mug over ice and top up with ginger beer.

GLASS TYPE:
MOSCOW MULE MUG

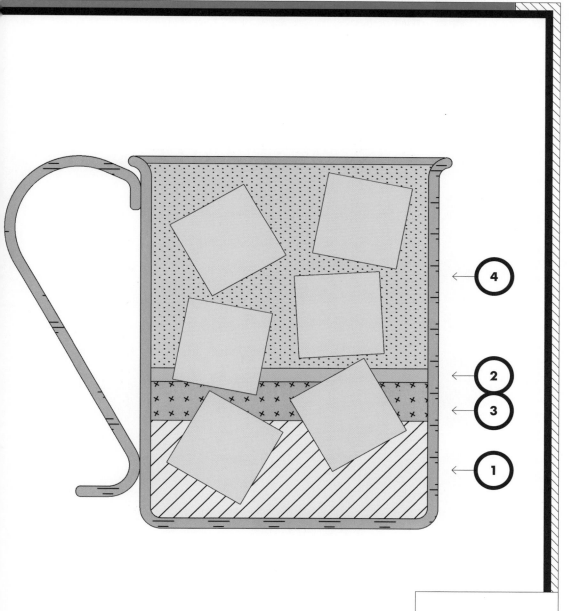

TIP Add a metal straw and 2–3 lime slices and stir until the mug is frosty.

DARK & STORMY

One of the finest ways to get tipsy on aged rum, this iconic, refreshing and rather simple concoction claims to be the national drink of Bermuda (in fact, many swear by Bermuda's own Gosling's Black Seal rum). Pour the rum in first for a perfect mix, or add it in last and let it seep through the ice for a little drama.

INGREDIENTS

1	aged rum	60 ml (2 oz)
2	lime juice, freshly squeezed	10 ml (2 tbsp)
3	ginger beer	to top up
4	lime slices	to garnish

EQUIPMENT

Bar spoon

METHOD

Fill a highball with ice, pour over the rum and lime juice, then top up with ginger beer. Stir and serve with lime slices.

GLASS TYPE:
HIGHBALL

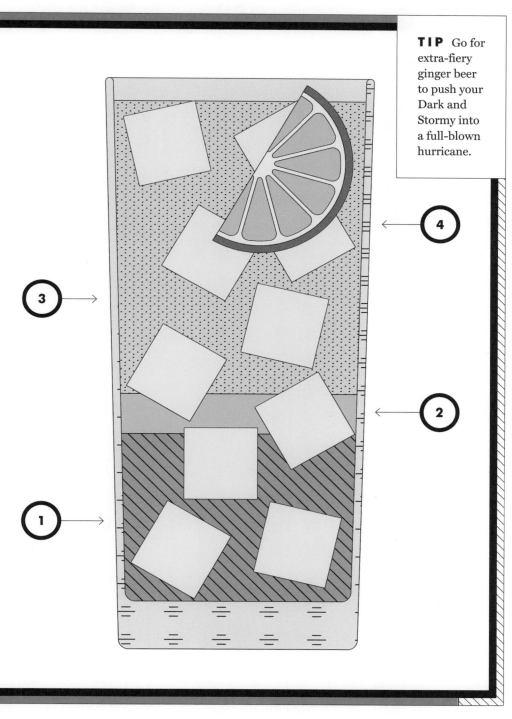

TIP Go for extra-fiery ginger beer to push your Dark and Stormy into a full-blown hurricane.

THE MANHATTAN

On the lips of partygoers since the late 1880s, New York City's infamous Manhattan Club crafted its signature cocktail with spicy American rye whiskey, sweet Italian vermouth, and a devil-may-care attitude. This ruby-hued bourbon version is just a little softer and sweeter. Can also be served on the rocks.

INGREDIENTS

1	bourbon	60 ml (2 oz)
2	red (sweet) vermouth	30 ml (1 oz)
3	Angostura bitters	2 dashes
4	orange bitters	1 dash
5	lemon twist	to garnish
6	cocktail cherry	to garnish

EQUIPMENT

Bar spoon, mixing glass, strainer

METHOD

Stir the ingredients in a mixing glass with ice to chill, strain into a chilled coupe and serve with a lemon twist and cocktail cherry.

GLASS TYPE:
CHILLED COUPE

TIP Garnish with a brandied cherry for extra booziness.

OLD FASHIONED

The world's most delicious way to drink bourbon, this recipe is carefully calibrated to underline the beauty and quality of the spirit. In this way, bourbon, rye, even mezcal or gin could be used; but rich, dark bourbon is best. Make sure your orange twist is big enough to whack into your nose as you sip for full sensory overload.

INGREDIENTS

1	brown sugar	1 cube
2	Angostura bitters	2 dashes
3	soda water	splash
4	bourbon	60 ml (2 oz)
5	cocktail cherry	to garnish
6	oversized orange twist	to garnish

EQUIPMENT

Muddler

METHOD

Add the sugar cube to the glass, wet with bitters and a splash of soda water, muddle until dissolved, add one or two large pieces of ice, then pour over the bourbon. Add a cocktail cherry, and bend a large orange twist over the drink to release a little fragrant citrus oil before adding to the drink.

GLASS TYPE:
HEAVY TUMBLER

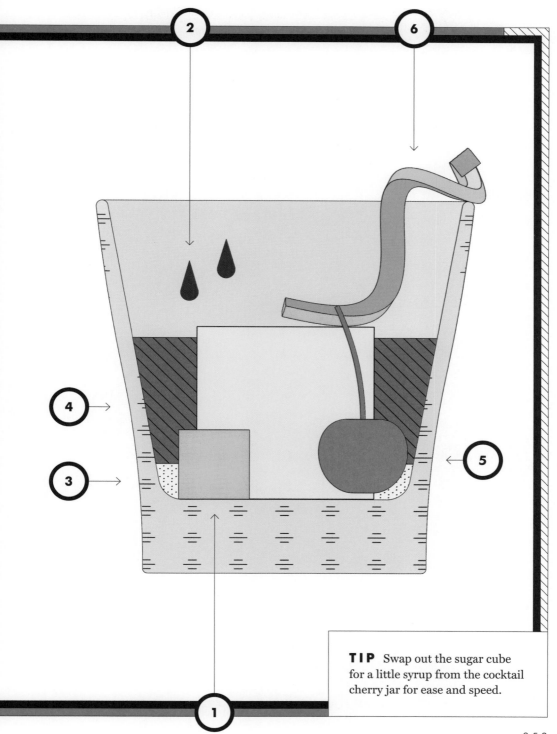

TIP Swap out the sugar cube for a little syrup from the cocktail cherry jar for ease and speed.

DIRTY MARTINI

This is one of the very best ways to drink gin: perfectly chilled, aromatic and underpinned with a little dry vermouth and the tang of brine. Use a good gourmet olive or caper berry and be generous with the brine. You should wince as it goes down. Absolutely filthy.

INGREDIENTS

1	gin	60 ml (2 oz)
2	dry vermouth	30 ml (1 oz)
3	olive brine	to taste
4	olives	to garnish

EQUIPMENT

Shaker, strainer

METHOD

Shake the gin and vermouth over ice, strain and pour into the glass. Spoon in the brine and add an olive or two.

GLASS TYPE:
MARTINI OR COUPE

TIP Swap out the olives for caper berries, cocktail onions, even cornichons if you're that way inclined.

LONG ISLAND ICED TEA

A cup of hot tea and a little drop of rum and vodka just seems, well, dirty. Throw out the tea and add a bucket of alcohol and ice and you apparently have yourself a rather classy, artful drink.

INGREDIENTS

1	white rum	30 ml (1 oz)
2	vodka	30 ml (1 oz)
3	gin	30 ml (1 oz)
4	tequila	30 ml (1 oz)
5	lemon juice, freshly squeezed	30 ml (1 oz)
6	orange liqueur	30 ml (1 oz)
7	Simple Syrup (page 29)	dash
8	lemon slice	to garnish
9	lime slice	to garnish

EQUIPMENT

Bar spoon, swizzle stick

METHOD

Pour the ingredients into a highball glass filled with ice cubes, stir, then add the lemon and lime slices. Serve with a swizzle stick and a couple of straws.

GLASS TYPE:
HIGHBALL

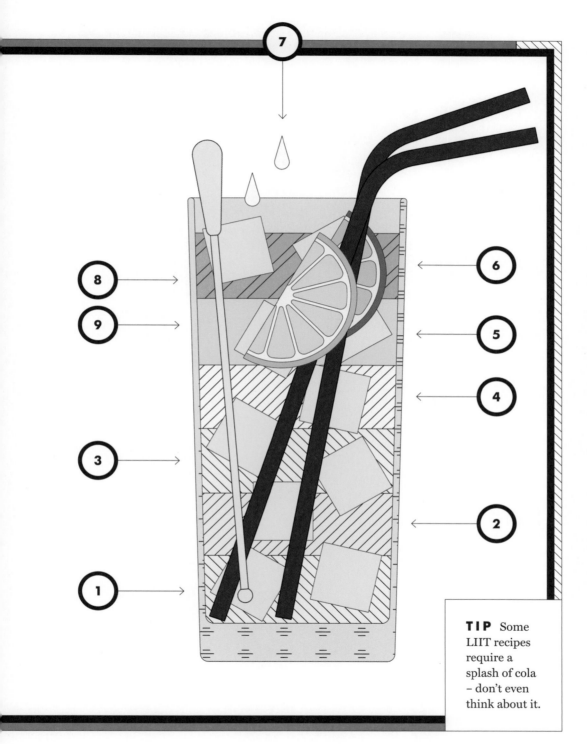

TIP Some LIIT recipes require a splash of cola – don't even think about it.

PALOMA

A fresh, zingy, almost-like-not-drinking-at-all way of drinking tequila. This long cocktail, topped with chilled soda water uses reposado as its base, pepped up with ruby grapefruit and lime juice. It's 100 per cent refreshing: no wonder it's Mexico's favourite tequila cocktail.

INGREDIENTS

1	reposado tequila	60 ml (2 oz)
2	ruby grapefruit juice, freshly squeezed	½ grapefruit
3	lime juice, freshly squeezed	15 ml (½ oz)
4	agave syrup (or Simple Syrup, page 29)	15 ml (½ oz)
5	soda water	to top up
6	lime wheel	to garnish

EQUIPMENT

Shaker, strainer

METHOD

Pour the tequila, juices and syrup into an ice-filled shaker. Shake vigorously and strain into an ice-filled glass. Top up with soda and garnish with a lime wheel.

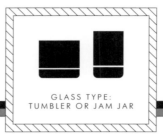

GLASS TYPE:
TUMBLER OR JAM JAR

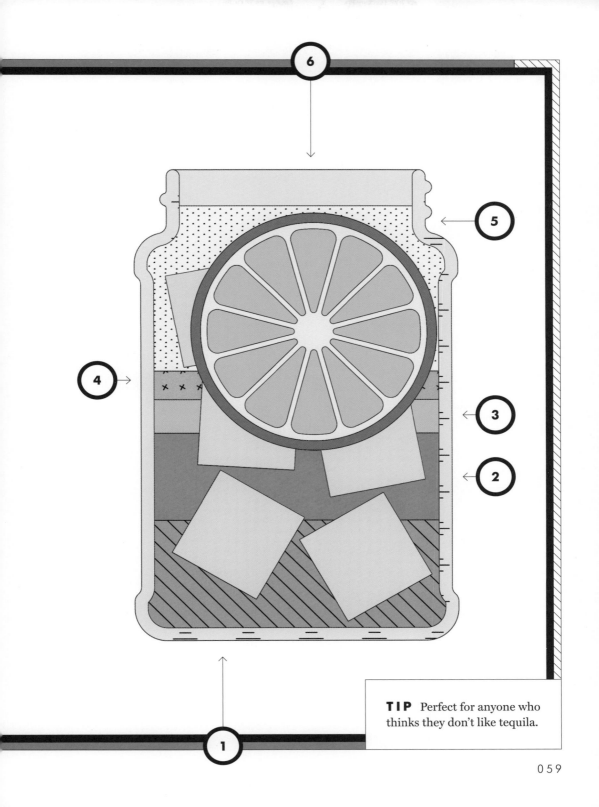

TIP Perfect for anyone who thinks they don't like tequila.

THE RATTLESNAKE

This once-forgotten classic is said to cure a rattlesnake bite – or kill the snake itself – and was first seen in print on London's Savoy Hotel cocktail list in 1930. It's a delightfully boozy drink that is tangy, sharp and creamy with an anise fragrance. It may not cure any emergency ailment whatsoever, but it will get you merry enough not to care.

INGREDIENTS

1	bourbon	45 ml (1½ oz)
2	egg white	1
3	lemon juice, freshly squeezed	dash
4	lime juice, freshly squeezed	dash
5	Simple Syrup (page 29)	10 ml (⅓ oz)
6	Pernod	to rinse

EQUIPMENT

Shaker, fine mesh sieve

METHOD

Dry shake the liquids (except the Pernod) until frothy. Then, add ice and shake again vigorously for a full 20 seconds. Rinse a chilled coupe with a quick splash of Pernod and discard. Strain through a fine mesh sieve and serve.

GLASS TYPE:
CHILLED COUPE

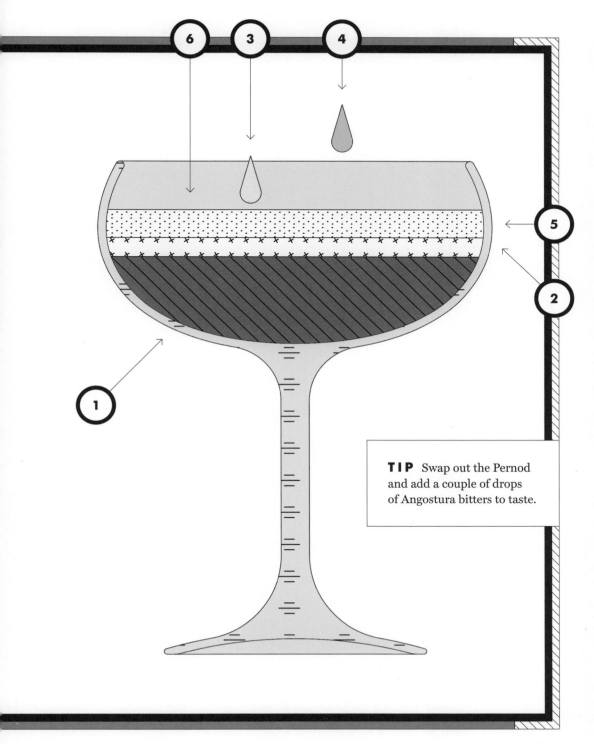

TIP Swap out the Pernod and add a couple of drops of Angostura bitters to taste.

THE GIBSON

This drink will put hairs on your chest. And onion on your breath. Think of it as a classic Martini soured with cocktail onions – try it with a little pickle juice if you're tough enough. Because of the simplicity of the recipe, pick a premium gin.

INGREDIENTS

1	gin	60 ml (2 oz)
2	dry vermouth	15 ml (½ oz)
3	cocktail onions	3, to garnish

EQUIPMENT
Shaker

METHOD
Shake the gin and dry vermouth over ice, pour into a chilled glass and add the cocktail onions.

GLASS TYPE:
MARTINI OR COUPE

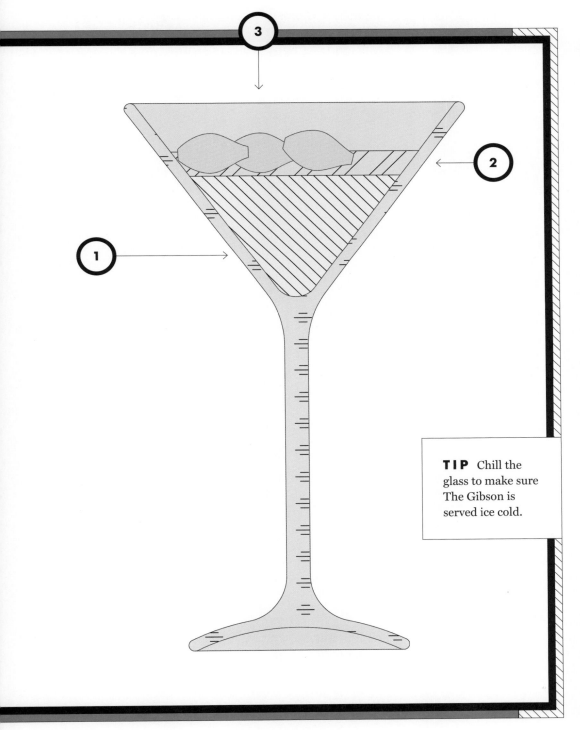

TIP Chill the glass to make sure The Gibson is served ice cold.

VODKA COLLINS

This classic cocktail lets the vodka sing. Use a premium spirit, super-fresh lemon juice, and – as this recipe is on the sweet side – feel free to tone down the syrup to taste.

INGREDIENTS

1	premium vodka	60 ml (2 oz)
2	lemon juice, freshly squeezed	30 ml (1 oz)
3	agave or Simple Syrup (page 29)	30 ml (1 oz)
4	chilled soda water	to top up
5	Angostura bitters	2 dashes

EQUIPMENT

Shaker, strainer

METHOD

Shake the vodka, lemon juice and syrup vigorously over ice. Strain into a coupe or flute and top up with chilled soda water. Add a couple of drops of Angostura bitters.

GLASS TYPE:
COUPE OR FLUTE

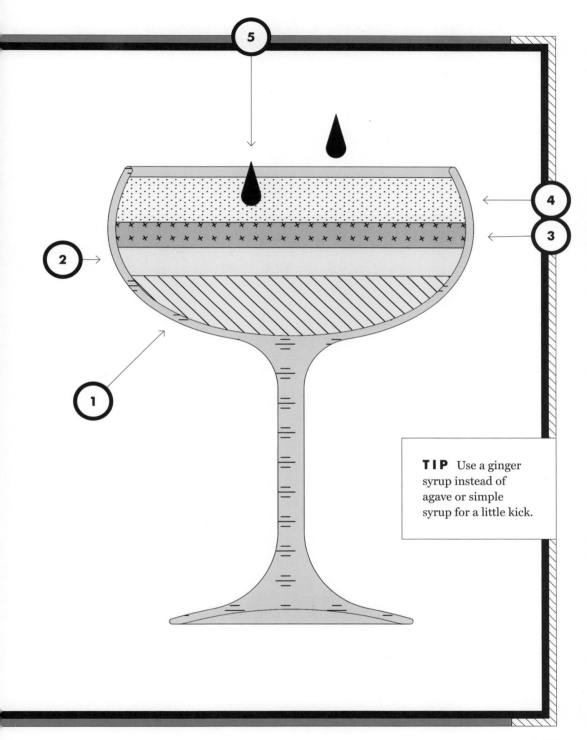

TIP Use a ginger syrup instead of agave or simple syrup for a little kick.

SEA BREEZE

Harking from the 1920s, the Sea Breeze has evolved from a simple gin and grenadine cocktail to this juicy and smooth vodka-powered classic.

INGREDIENTS

1	premium vodka	60 ml (2 oz)
2	grapefruit juice, freshly squeezed	150 ml (5 oz)
3	cranberry juice	100 ml (3½ oz)
4	lime juice, freshly squeezed	½ lime
5	lime wheel	to garnish
6	citrus bitters	2 dashes

METHOD

Add the ingredients to a glass filled with ice in the order above (pour gently to create an ombré effect). Garnish with the lime wheel and top with the bitters.

GLASS TYPE:
BOSTON
OR HIGHBALL

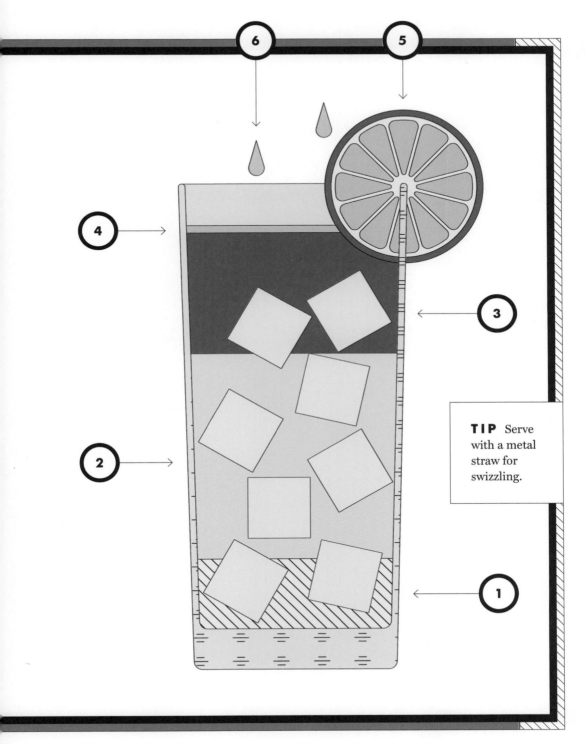

TIP Serve with a metal straw for swizzling.

THE SAZERAC

This heady New Orleans cocktail is a twist on the classic Old Fashioned but with booze brand Sazerac's own anise-powered Peychaud's bitters, cognac and a little absinthe for summoning the spirit world. This 19th century concoction is a strong, complex herbal drink for late night scrying and spellcasting. Stiff AF.

INGREDIENTS

1	brown sugar	1 cube
2	Peychaud's bitters	2 dashes
3	Angostura bitters	1 dash
4	bourbon or rye	30 ml (1 oz)
5	cognac	30 ml (1 oz)
6	absinthe	to rinse glass
7	lemon twist	to garnish

EQUIPMENT

Muddler, mixing glass, strainer

METHOD

Muddle the sugar, bitters and a dash of water in a mixing glass, add the bourbon, cognac and ice, and stir until frosty. Rinse a chilled tumbler with absinthe, discard the excess. Add one or two large pieces of ice and strain drink into glass. Garnish with a lemon twist.

GLASS TYPE:
HEAVY TUMBLER

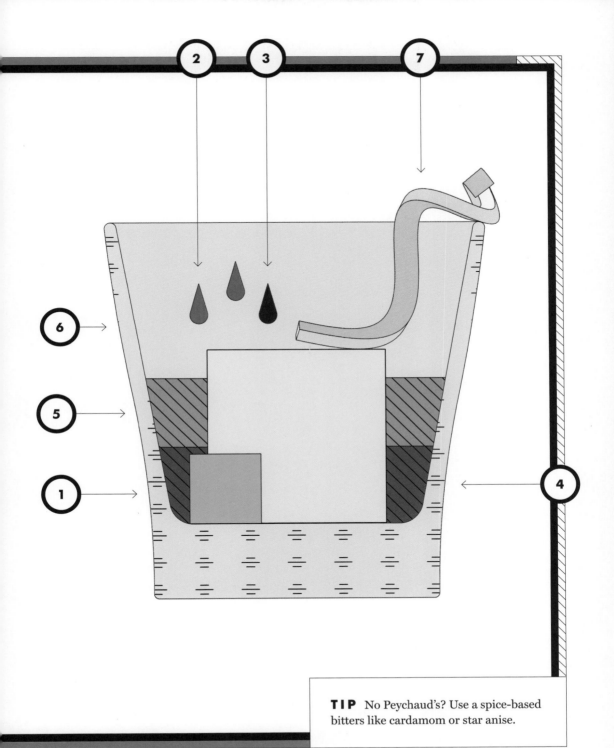

TIP No Peychaud's? Use a spice-based bitters like cardamom or star anise.

SEX ON THE BEACH

Because, why not? This classic may have the most cringe-inducing name in the cocktail world, but it's supremely delicious. Slip on your SPF and enjoy sex on the beach, but without the sand in your gusset.

INGREDIENTS

1	vodka	45 ml (1½ oz)
2	peach liqueur	15 ml (½ oz)
3	smooth orange juice	60 ml (2 oz)
4	cranberry juice	60 ml (2 oz)
5	lime wheel	to garnish
6	maraschino cherry	to garnish

METHOD

Fill a highball glass with ice cubes, add the liquids in the order above (pour gently to create an orange-to-red ombré effect) and top with a lime wheel slice and maraschino cherry for a little retro touch.

GLASS TYPE:
HIGHBALL

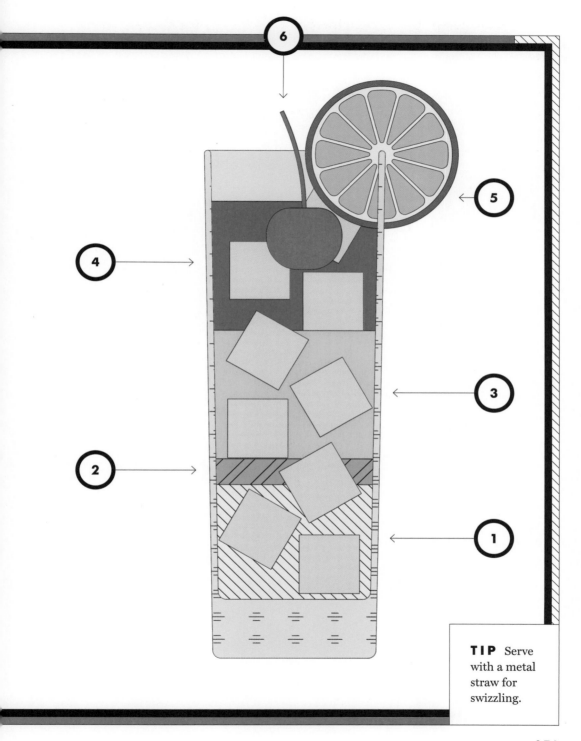

TIP Serve with a metal straw for swizzling.

TEQUILA SUNRISE

One sip of a Tequila Sunrise, with its novelty colour gradient from orange to blood-red and cherry, is like time travelling back to the 1980s. Drink with big hair, frosted eye shadow and the soundtrack to *Cocktail* on repeat.

INGREDIENTS

1	gold tequila	45 ml (1½ oz)
2	orange juice, freshly squeezed	90 ml (3 oz)
3	grenadine	dash
4	orange wheel	to garnish
5	speared maraschino cherry	to garnish

EQUIPMENT

Bar spoon

METHOD

Fill a glass with ice, pour over the tequila and orange juice and stir gently with a bar spoon. Gently drop the grenadine onto the top so that it sinks down through the drink. Garnish with an orange wheel and a speared cherry.

GLASS TYPE:
COLLINS

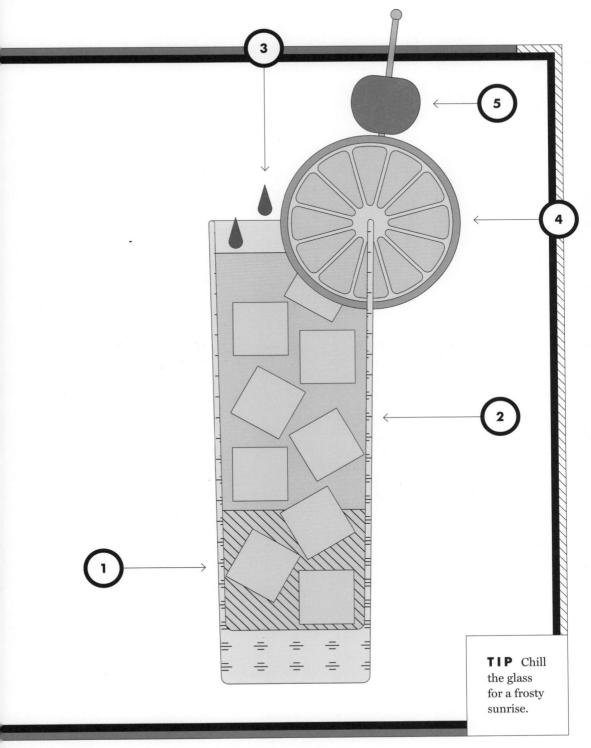

TIP Chill the glass for a frosty sunrise.

The Reinventions

Classic cocktails reworked for modern times.
We've rammed a pineapple into a mule
and reworked the classic spritz. Like all the best
things in life, all you need is a little twist.

075

SPICED GINGER NEGRONI

A spiced, rum-powered update of the classic ruby-red and bitter-sweet cocktail. The spiced rum, underlined by zesty ginger liqueur (The King's Ginger by Berry Bros & Rudd is the most iconic), gives a dark, complex feel – it's still a dry, sharp Negroni, but not as you know it.

INGREDIENTS

1	spiced rum	60 ml (2 oz)
2	Aperol	60 ml (2 oz)
3	ginger liqueur	30 ml (1 oz)
4	sweet vermouth	30 ml (1 oz)
5	orange twist	to garnish

EQUIPMENT

Bar spoon, mixing glass, strainer

METHOD

Stir the liquids over a few cubes of ice in a mixing glass; add more ice and repeat. Strain into a chilled tumbler with a large rock of ice. Garnish with the orange twist.

GLASS TYPE:
TUMBLER

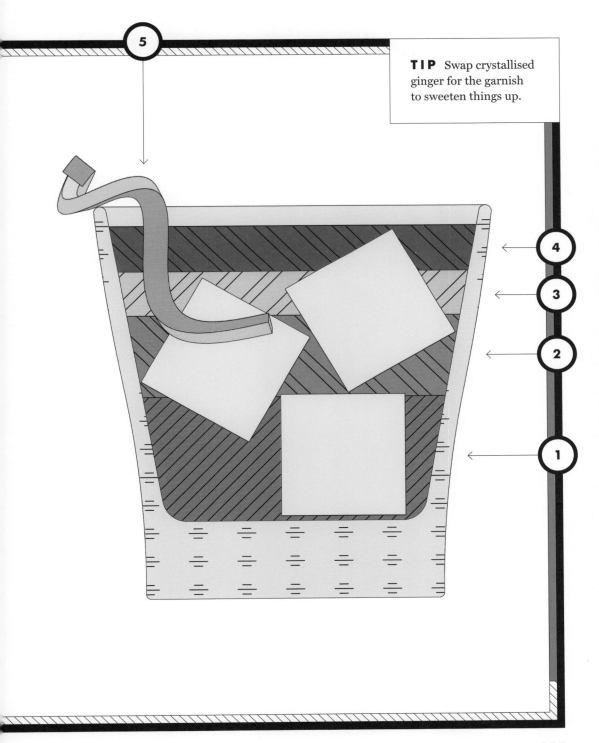

TIP Swap crystallised ginger for the garnish to sweeten things up.

BERGAMOT TEA MARTINI

Temperature is essential for this one – the iciness will mellow out the spirits and lift the bergamot oil-infused tea leaves to new heights. Keep it classy; otherwise, it's just a couple of shots of booze with a teabag thrown in. It's all in the eye of the beholder.

INGREDIENTS

1	{	gin	30 ml (1 oz)
2	{	vodka	30 ml (1 oz)
3	{	premium Earl Grey teabag	1
4	{	orange bitters	dash
5	{	orange twist	to garnish

EQUIPMENT

Shaker

METHOD

Pour the gin and vodka over a premium Earl Grey teabag at room temperature, allow to steep for 30 minutes, then remove the teabag. Add the bitters, shake vigorously over ice, then strain into a mug and serve with orange twist to garnish.

GLASS TYPE:
MUG

TIP Chill your glass; this is best served super chilled.

SPICED RHUBARB & ROSE RAMOS GIN FIZZ

Inspired by legendary cocktail maker Henry C. Ramos, who created the Ramos Gin Fizz in New Orleans, 1888, this is perhaps the campest cocktail in the book. This pastel pink drink – with its delicately perfumed aroma – is unashamedly delicious. It's like a scantily clad slumber party in a glass.

INGREDIENTS

1	gin	60 ml (2 oz)
2	Rhubarb, Ginger and Star Anise Syrup (see flavoured syrup method, page 31)	60 ml (2 oz)
3	single (light) cream	30 ml (1 oz)
4	lime juice, freshly squeezed	15 ml (½ oz)
5	lemon juice, freshly squeezed	15 ml (½ oz)
6	egg white	1
7	rosewater	dash
8	chilled soda water	to top up

EQUIPMENT

Shaker, strainer

METHOD

Shake the liquids – except the soda water – for 30 seconds, then add ice and shake for a further 30 seconds. Strain into a coupe filled with ice cubes and top with chilled soda water.

GLASS TYPE:
COUPE

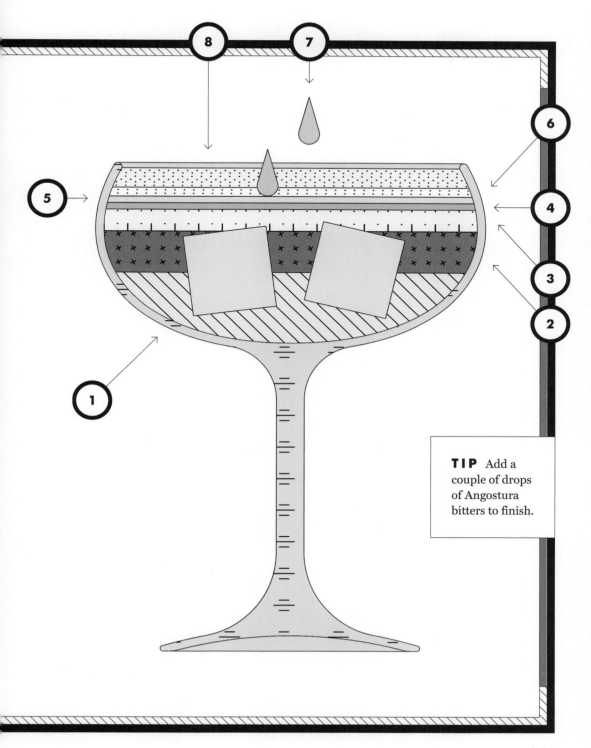

TIP Add a couple of drops of Angostura bitters to finish.

BAY LEAF & GREEN TEA MARTINI

The classic Martini, underpinned with an excellent, high-quality and super-dry gin, with a bay and green tea flavour adding a fresh, verdant and rather firm woodiness.

INGREDIENTS

1	premium green teabag	1
2	vodka	30 ml (1 oz)
3	Bay Leaf Gin (see flavoured syrup method, page 31)	60 ml (2 oz)
4	lemon juice, freshly squeezed	15 ml (½ oz)
5	fresh bay leaf	to garnish

EQUIPMENT

Shaker, strainer

METHOD

Steep the green teabag in the vodka and gin at room temperature for at least 30 minutes. Add the lemon juice and shake over ice, then strain into a martini glass or coupe. Garnish with a bay leaf.

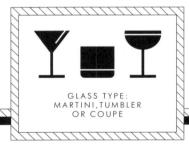

GLASS TYPE:
MARTINI, TUMBLER
OR COUPE

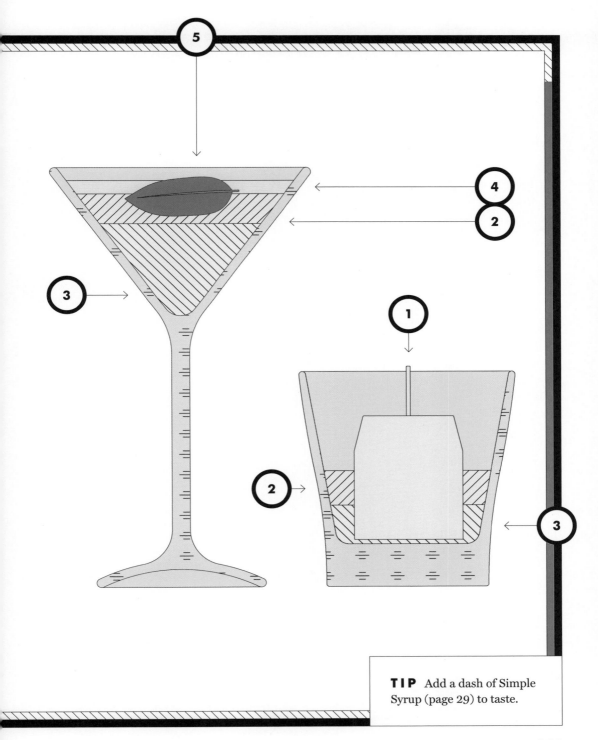

TIP Add a dash of Simple Syrup (page 29) to taste.

PINEAPPLE MOSCOW MULE

A pineapple-powered Mule with a tiki twist: a tropical version of the classic 1940s vodka cocktail.

INGREDIENTS

1	premium vodka	60 ml (2 oz)
2	pineapple juice	60 ml (2 oz)
3	lime juice, freshly squeezed	½ lime
4	chilled ginger beer	to top up
5	lime wedges	to garnish

EQUIPMENT

Shaker, strainer

METHOD

Shake the vodka, pineapple and lime juices with ice. Strain into a Moscow mule mug over ice and top up with ginger beer. Garnish with lime wedges.

GLASS TYPE:
MOSCOW MULE
MUG

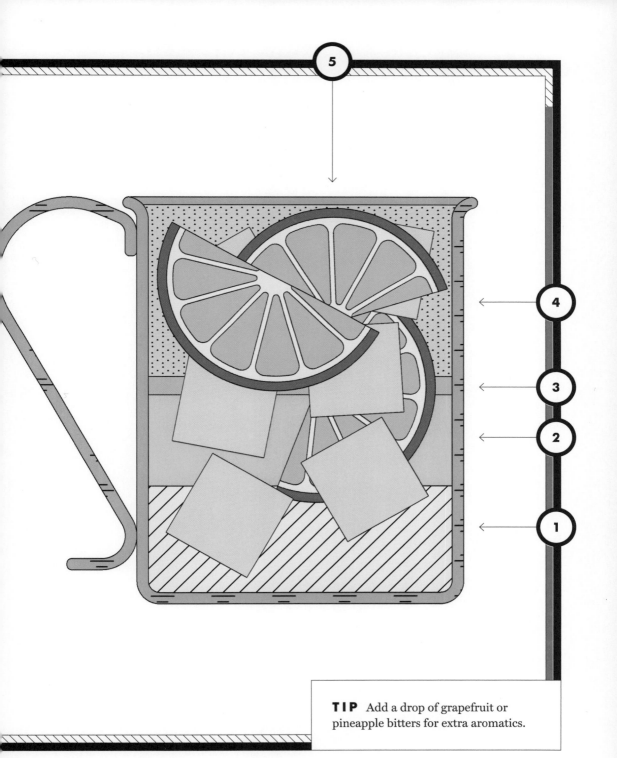

TIP Add a drop of grapefruit or pineapple bitters for extra aromatics.

BEVERLY HILLS ICED TEA

A luxury version of the classic cocktail, swapping the quaint fishing villages of the New York State coastline for the sunshine glamour of Beverly Hills. This version is powered by smooth premium vodka and topped with chilled Champagne.

INGREDIENTS

1	premium vodka	15 ml (½ oz)
2	gold tequila	15 ml (½ oz)
3	gold rum	15 ml (½ oz)
4	gin	15 ml (½ oz)
5	triple sec	15 ml (½ oz)
6	Sweet & Sour Mix (page 30)	30 ml (1 oz)
7	chilled Champagne	to top up
8	lemon wedge	to garnish

EQUIPMENT

Shaker, strainer

METHOD

Pour all of the ingredients (except the Champagne and lemon wedge) into a shaker filled with ice. Shake until cold and frothy, then strain into a chilled glass filled with ice. Top up with Champagne and squeeze a lemon wedge on top.

GLASS TYPE:
COLLINS

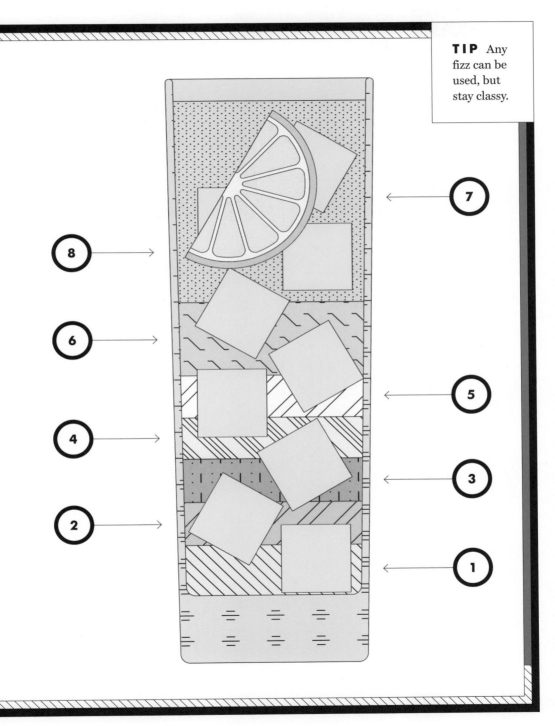

NEW CLASSICO SPRITZ

The non-classic take on the traditional Spritz that's becoming a classic in its own right. Try using Contratto Bitter in favour of Campari or Aperol (although all three work beautifully) and get used to your new default summer drink.

INGREDIENTS

1	vodka	30 ml (1 oz)
2	Aperol or other bitter liqueur	30 ml (1 oz)
3	St-Germain elderflower liqueur	15 ml (½ oz)
4	grapefruit juice, freshly squeezed	25 ml (¾ oz)
5	chilled prosecco	to top up

METHOD

Add vodka, Aperol, elderflower liqueur and grapefruit juice to a glass over ice, top up with chilled prosecco and serve with a straw.

GLASS TYPE: WINE,
TUMBLER OR HIGHBALL

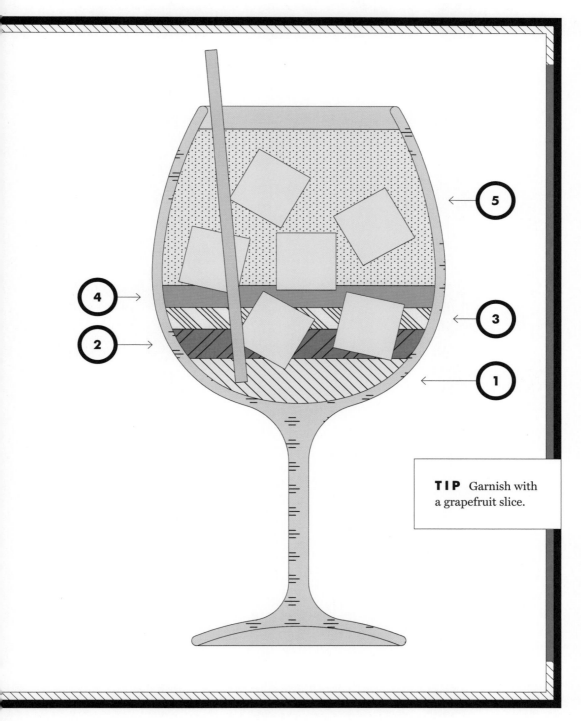

TIP Garnish with a grapefruit slice.

RHUBARB MOJITO

A ruby-red edition of the Cuban classic, where the tropical taste of white rum, sugar, mint, sharp lime and soda water is given a hot rhubarb injection; the unexpected taste of the English kitchen garden, if you will. The zingy rhubarb gives the Mojito a rich depth without losing the fizzing, citrus taste.

INGREDIENTS

1	lime wedges	2
2	demerara sugar	2 tsp
3	fresh mint leaves	12
4	white rum	60 ml (2 oz)
5	Rhubarb and Star Anise Syrup (see flavoured syrup method, page 31)	2 tbsp
6	chilled soda water	to top up
7	fresh mint sprig	to garnish

EQUIPMENT

Muddler

METHOD

Muddle the lime wedges and sugar in the highball, going hard for more citrus flavour or gentle for a subtler taste. Add the mint leaves and gently muddle, then fill the glass three-quarters full with crushed ice, add the rum and syrup and stir. Finally, add more crushed ice, top with chilled soda water and a mint sprig.

GLASS TYPE:
HIGHBALL

TIP Every evening, my dad used to water his rhubarb in an unusual way: make sure you wash yours before cooking.

HARD CIDER

Created for Americans who tend to forget to put alcohol in their cider, this delicious, smoky-sweet cloudy cocktail has a fresh, herby countryside taste and a mule's kick of aged rum. Don't scrimp on the maple syrup and use the best (i.e. not the McDonald's pancake syrup you stockpile in your desk drawer).

INGREDIENTS

1	aged rum	60 ml (2 oz)
2	cloudy apple juice	120 ml (4 oz)
3	maple syrup	2 tbsp
4	lemon juice, freshly squeezed	dash
5	fresh thyme sprigs	1

EQUIPMENT

Shaker

METHOD

Shake the liquids and a sprig of thyme (bruised) over ice until frosty. Serve with a fresh thyme sprig.

GLASS TYPE:
COUPE

TIP Make sure you use good quality apple juice, not the clear juicebox type.

RASPBERRY COSMOPOLITAN

A contemporary version that blows a raspberry at the pink, sharp, vodka-based cocktail that dominated 90s cocktail culture. It's a shade sweeter than the classic Cosmo, but remains dry enough for the cocktail purists.

INGREDIENTS

1	Absolut Citron vodka	50 ml (1¾ oz)
2	triple sec	15 ml (½ oz)
3	crème de raspberry	15 ml (½ oz)
4	cranberry juice	25 ml (¾ oz)
5	raspberry	to garnish

EQUIPMENT

Shaker, strainer

METHOD

Shake the liquids with ice and strain into a chilled martini glass or coupe. Garnish with a raspberry and serve.

GLASS TYPE:
MARTINI OR COUPE

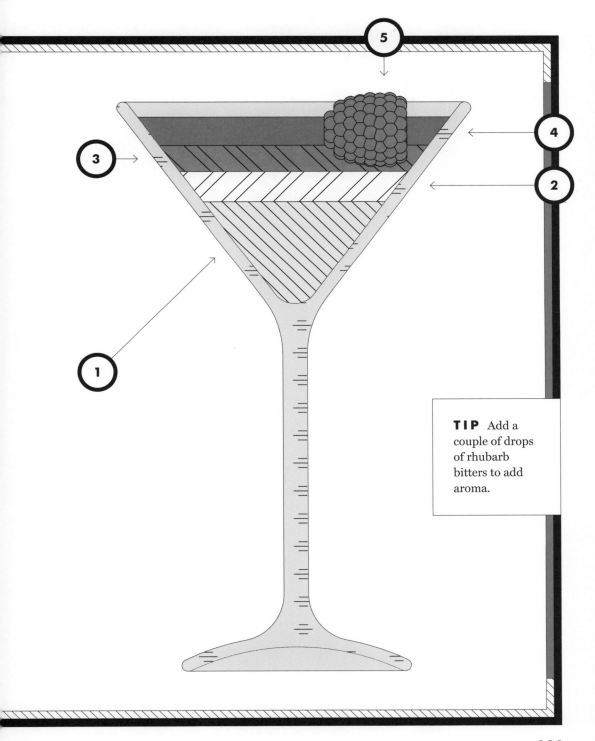

TIP Add a couple of drops of rhubarb bitters to add aroma.

CHERRY FRENCH 75

This drink combines two wonderful things: being French and an obsession with cherry popping. This classic cocktail, with a fruity upgrade, is fresh and sharp with a little fizz for good measure.

INGREDIENTS

1	ripe, stoned small cherries	handful
2	Cherry Heering liqueur	15 ml (½ oz)
3	lemon juice, freshly squeezed	15 ml (½ oz)
4	rosewater	dash
5	gin	60 ml (2 oz)
6	chilled prosecco	to top up
7	cherry	to garnish

EQUIPMENT

Muddler, shaker, strainer

METHOD

Gently muddle the cherries, Cherry Heering, lemon juice and rosewater. Add the gin and shake over ice. Strain into a martini glass or coupe and top with chilled prosecco. Garnish with a single cherry.

GLASS TYPE:
COUPE OR MARTINI

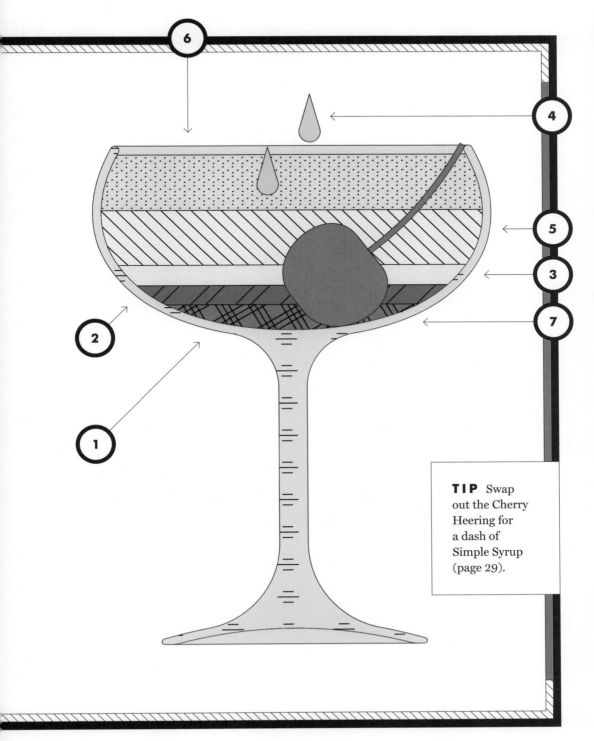

TIP Swap out the Cherry Heering for a dash of Simple Syrup (page 29).

Citrus
& Sours

Booze and citrus: the finest bedfellows. Fresh squeezings of lime, lemon and grapefruit and pungent, aromatic peel garnishes elevate your favourite spirits to another plane. From the delicately sharp Grapefruit Tarragon Collins to the perfect Whisky Sour.

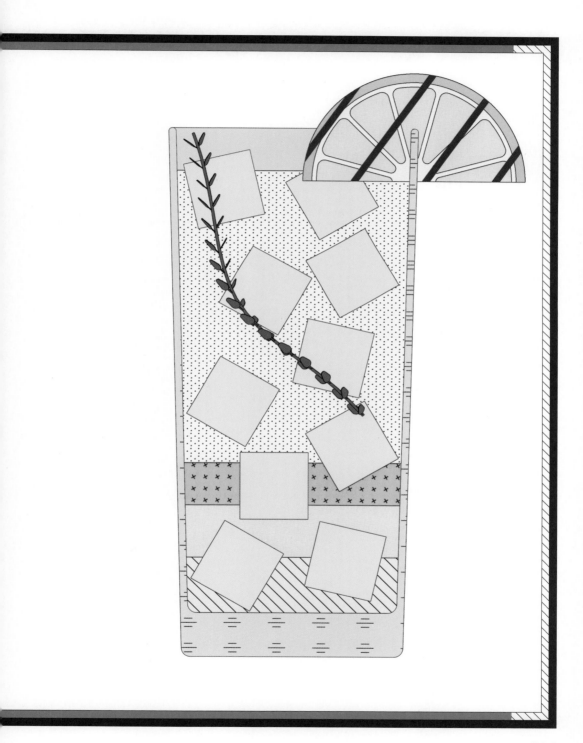

GIN RICKEY

Simple, sharp, refreshing and – after a couple – dizzying. Tweak the balance between sugar and lime to taste, but a good Rickey should be bright, sharp and strong.

INGREDIENTS

1	gin	60 ml (2 oz)
2	lime juice, freshly squeezed	1 tbsp
3	Simple Syrup (page 29)	1 tbsp
4	soda water	to top up
5	lime wedge	to garnish

METHOD

Pour the gin, lime juice and syrup into a coupe filled with ice cubes. Top up with soda water and garnish with a lime wedge.

GLASS TYPE:
COUPE

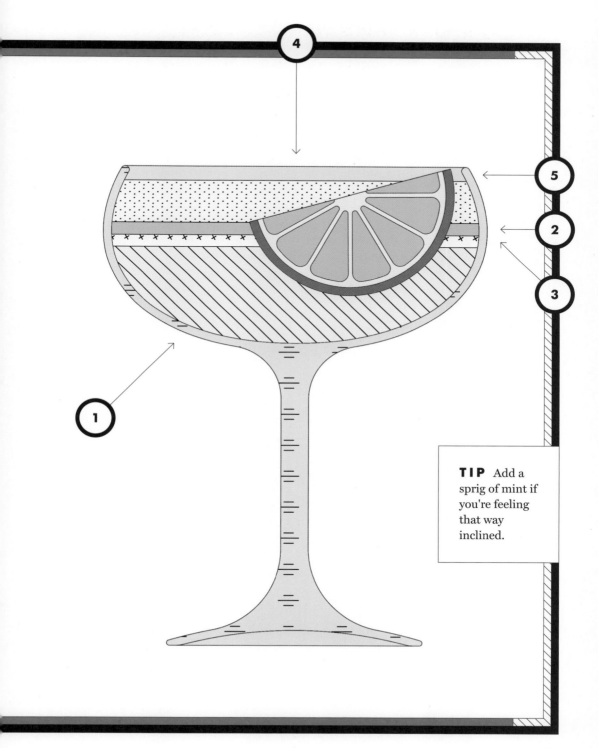

TIP Add a sprig of mint if you're feeling that way inclined.

GRAPEFRUIT & TARRAGON COLLINS

The classic Gin Collins reworked with the soft anise flavour of fresh tarragon and the sharp tang of grapefruit. The grapefruit lends a soft pink tone and the tarragon adds a herby, liquorice aroma.

INGREDIENTS

1	fresh tarragon	3–4 leaves
2	light brown sugar	1 tsp
3	gin	60 ml (2 oz)
4	pink or ruby grapefruit juice	60 ml (2 oz)
5	chilled tonic water	to top up
6	fresh tarragon	to garnish
7	grapefruit twist	to garnish

EQUIPMENT

Muddler, shaker, strainer

METHOD

Muddle the fresh tarragon and sugar in a shaker. Add a handful of ice cubes, the gin and grapefruit juice, shake and strain into a collins glass full of ice. Top with chilled tonic water. Add a few leaves of tarragon and grapefruit twist to garnish.

GLASS TYPE:
COLLINS

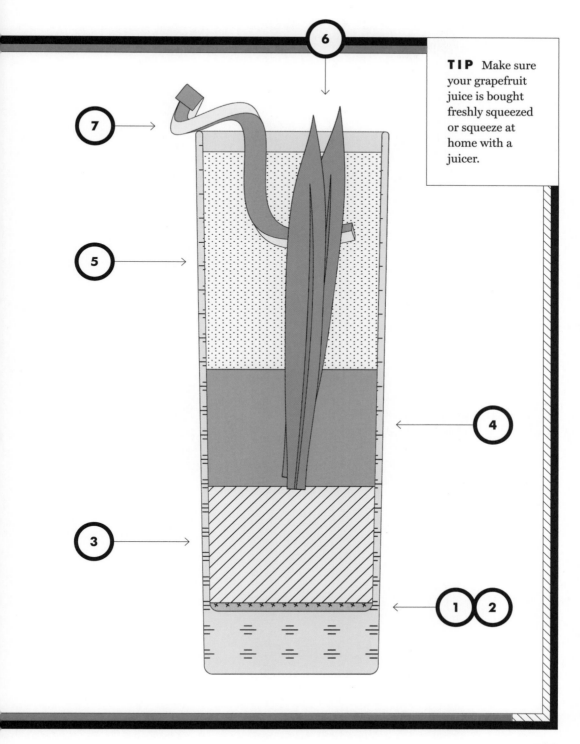

GIMLET

The original gin and juice – a power-punch of a cocktail. You can swap the lime juice for any other acidic fruit.

INGREDIENTS

1	}	gin	60 ml (2 oz)
2	}	lime juice, freshly squeezed	15 ml (½ oz)

EQUIPMENT

Shaker, strainer

METHOD

Shake the ingredients with ice and vigour and strain into a chilled martini glass or coupe with a couple of ice cubes.

GLASS TYPE:
COUPE OR MARTINI

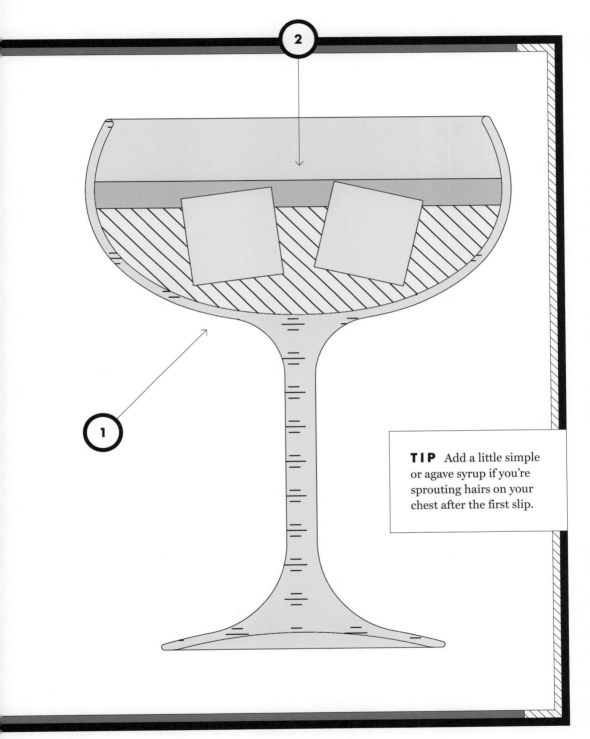

TIP Add a little simple or agave syrup if you're sprouting hairs on your chest after the first slip.

WHISKY SOUR

This classic short drink perfectly straddles the sweet-sour binary with sharp citrus flavour and sweet simple syrup that will liven up anything from your favourite premium bourbon to whatever firewater you nab on a late night booze run. It has an easy-on-the-eye orange hue and is drinkable in the extreme. Serve icy cold, of course.

INGREDIENTS

1	bourbon	60ml (2 oz)
2	lemon juice, freshly squeezed	20 ml (⅔ oz)
3	Simple Syrup (page 29)	20 ml (⅔ oz)
4	orange wheel	½, to garnish
5	maraschino cherry	to garnish

EQUIPMENT

Shaker, strainer

METHOD

Shake the bourbon, lemon juice and simple syrup over ice until very cold. Strain into a glass filled with ice, add garnish and serve.

GLASS TYPE:
TUMBLER OR
ROCKS GLASS

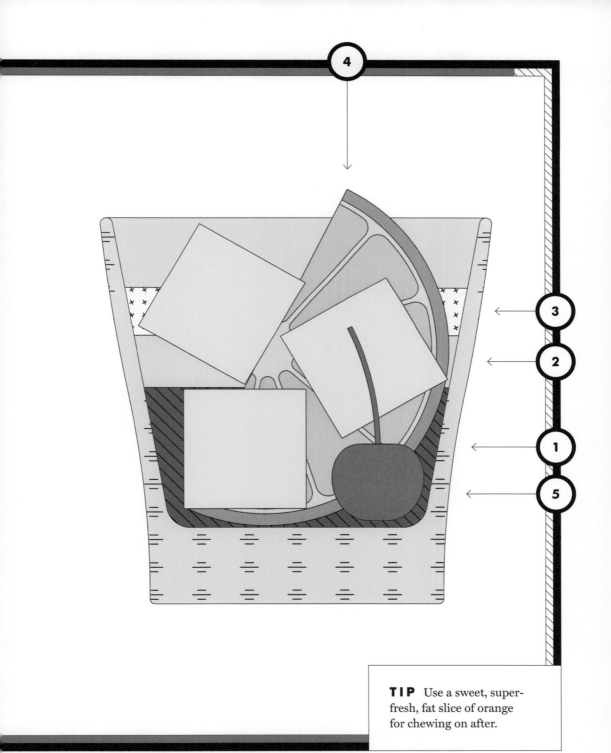

TIP Use a sweet, super-fresh, fat slice of orange for chewing on after.

BREAKFAST MARGARITA

Struggling to balance your love of toasted sliced sourdough and zingy citrus preserve with living your best gluten-free life? Swap out the bread for tequila. This Margie kick-starts boozy brunches and post-night out recovery sessions. Worth setting your alarm clock for.

INGREDIENTS

1	reposado tequila	45 ml (1½ oz)
2	orange liqueur	22.5 ml (¾ oz)
3	lime juice, freshly squeezed	22.5 ml (¾ oz)
4	orange marmalade	1 heaped tsp
5	Simple Syrup (page 29)	7.5 ml (¼ oz)
6	orange twist	to garnish

EQUIPMENT

Shaker, strainer

METHOD

Add all of the ingredients (except the garnish) to an ice-filled shaker and shake until cold. Strain into an ice-filled glass and add an orange twist.

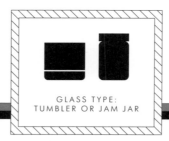

GLASS TYPE:
TUMBLER OR JAM JAR

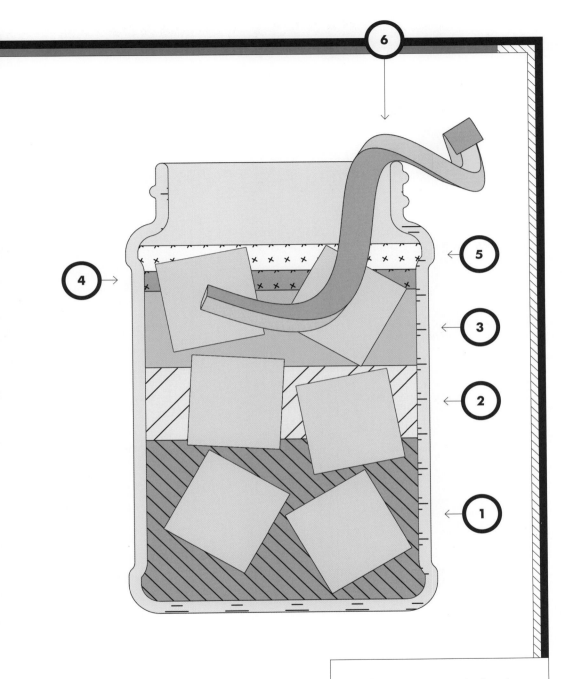

TIP Blend with ice (rather than shake) for an icy breakfast blast.

RHUBARB SOUR

A small, delicately pink and frothy cocktail that slaps you in the face with its tangy sour-sweetness. The acidic-stalked rhubarb plant is a mainstay of many an English garden, as are hedgehogs (they're not needed here – they taste awful).

INGREDIENTS

1	gin	60 ml (2 oz)
2	triple sec	30 ml (1 oz)
3	lemon juice, freshly squeezed	30 ml (1 oz)
4	Rhubarb Syrup (see flavoured syrup method, page 31)	120 ml (4 oz)
5	egg white	1
6	orange twist	to garnish

EQUIPMENT

Shaker, strainer

METHOD

Shake the gin, triple sec, lemon juice, rhubarb syrup and egg white vigorously over ice. Strain into a coupe and garnish with orange twist.

GLASS TYPE:
COUPE

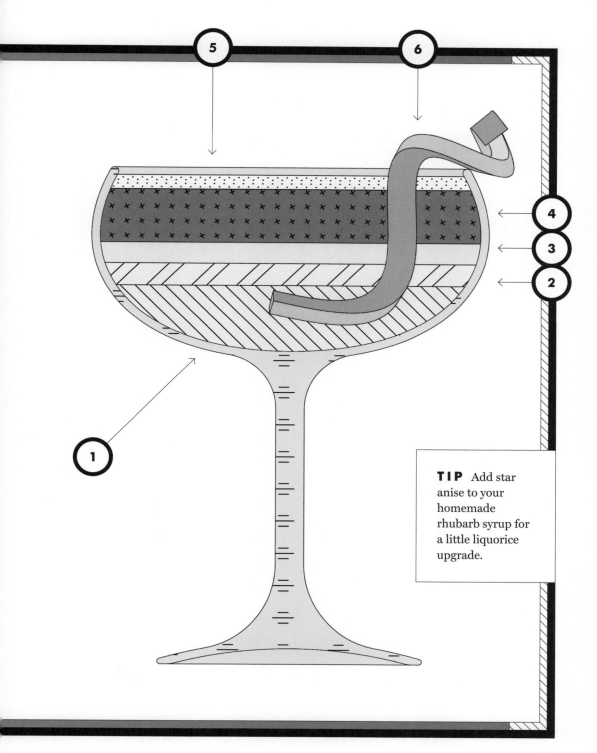

FROZEN BLOOD ORANGE MARGARITA

This dark pink, slushie-style drink is *muy* delicious, and blending until smooth makes this the easiest, speediest way to mainline a Margie – plus, the orange juice is one of your five-a-day.

INGREDIENTS

1	lime wedge	for salt rim
2	sea salt	for salt rim
3	silver tequila	45 ml (1½ oz)
4	triple sec	15 ml (½ oz)
5	blood orange juice, freshly squeezed	60 ml (2 oz)
6	agave syrup	15 ml (½ oz)
7	lime juice	dash

EQUIPMENT

Blender, saucer for salt rim

METHOD

Squish a lime wedge along the edge of a chilled glass and dip in sea salt. Add all the ingredients (except the lime juice) into a blender with a scoop of crushed ice. Blend on high speed until smooth. Pour into your glass and top with a dash of lime juice.

GLASS TYPE:
MARGARITA OR
LARGE WINE

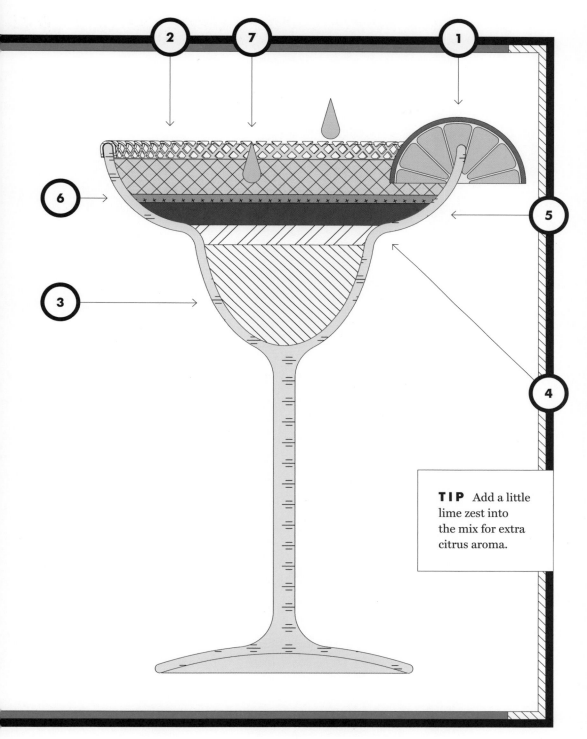

TIP Add a little lime zest into the mix for extra citrus aroma.

GRAPEFRUIT RIVERA

Lightly bitter grapefruit balanced with sweet and fragrant elderflower, underpinned with a wallop of premium vodka. A fragile-looking concoction that hides a real strength.

INGREDIENTS

1	premium vodka	60 ml (2 oz)
2	St-Germain elderflower liqueur	30 ml (1 oz)
3	pink grapefruit juice, freshly squeezed	50 ml (1¾ oz)

EQUIPMENT

Shaker, strainer

METHOD

Shake all the ingredients with ice until frosty and strain into a chilled glass.

GLASS TYPE:
COUPE OR MARTINI

TIP A drop of Angostura bitters before serving adds a dark, aromatic swirl.

CHARRED LEMONADE

This smoky, honey-sweet, fresh citrus long drink is hands-down delicious. Use a premium or a lemon- or mandarin-infused vodka, sweet honey syrup and the freshest, most squidgy lemons you can find.

INGREDIENTS

1	lemons	2–3
2	premium vodka	30 ml (1 oz)
3	Honey Syrup (see flavoured syrup method, page 31)	30 ml (1 oz)
4	chilled soda water	to top up
5	fresh thyme sprig	to garnish
6	lemon slice	to garnish

EQUIPMENT

Mixing glass, griddle pan

METHOD

Halve the lemons and char, flesh-side down, on a hot griddle pan for until lightly charred (less than a minute), then for the garnish char a lemon slice for 20 seconds or so. Juice the lemon halves and add 30 ml (1 oz) of the liquid plus the vodka and honey syrup to a mixing glass with ice. Stir until frosty, add to a highball glass with ice and a thyme sprig and top up with soda. Garnish with the charred lemon slice.

GLASS TYPE:
HIGHBALL

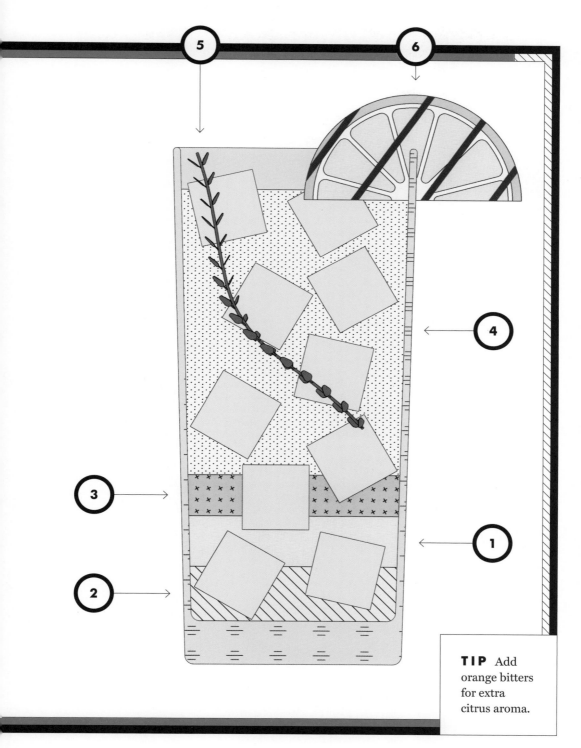

TIP Add orange bitters for extra citrus aroma.

YUZU GINGER DAIQUIRI

The Japanese citrus fruit, yuzu (sharp, like a grapefruit), is perhaps unaware of its current culinary trendiness, but – with fresh clementine juice – it gives real citrus power to this delicious, tangy and fragrant daiquiri with a spicy and sweet ginger undertone.

INGREDIENTS

1	white rum	60 ml (2 oz)
2	lime juice, freshly squeezed	15 ml (½ oz)
3	Ginger Syrup (see flavoured syrup method, page 31)	10 ml (⅓ oz)
4	clementine juice, freshly squeezed	30 ml (1 oz)
5	yuzu juice, freshly squeezed if possible	dash
6	chilled sparkling water	to top up
7	orange twist	to garnish

EQUIPMENT

Shaker, strainer

METHOD

Fill a shaker with crushed ice. Add the rum, lime juice, ginger syrup, clementine juice and yuzu juice, then shake with all your might until frothy. Strain into a chilled glass, top up with chilled sparkling water and garnish with an orange twist.

GLASS TYPE:
COUPE

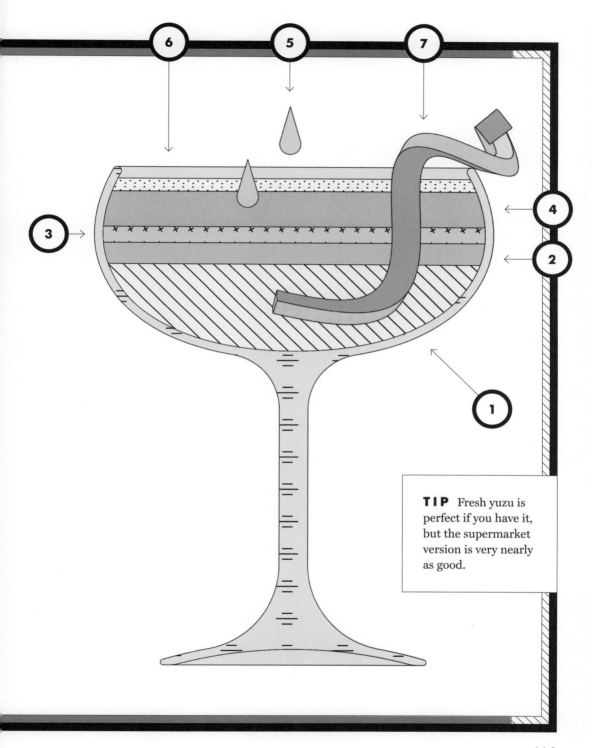

PINK RIVERA

As with the Grapefruit Rivera (page 114), sharp grapefruit is balanced with fragrant elderflower – but here with the addition of a smooth, vanilla undertone from the rum. Delicious, but dangerous.

INGREDIENTS

1	light rum	60 ml (2 oz)
2	St-Germain elderflower liqueur	30 ml (1 oz)
3	pink grapefruit juice, freshly squeezed	50 ml (1¾ oz)

EQUIPMENT

Shaker, strainer

METHOD

Add all the ingredients to a shaker. Shake over ice until frosty, then strain into a chilled coupe.

GLASS TYPE:
COUPE

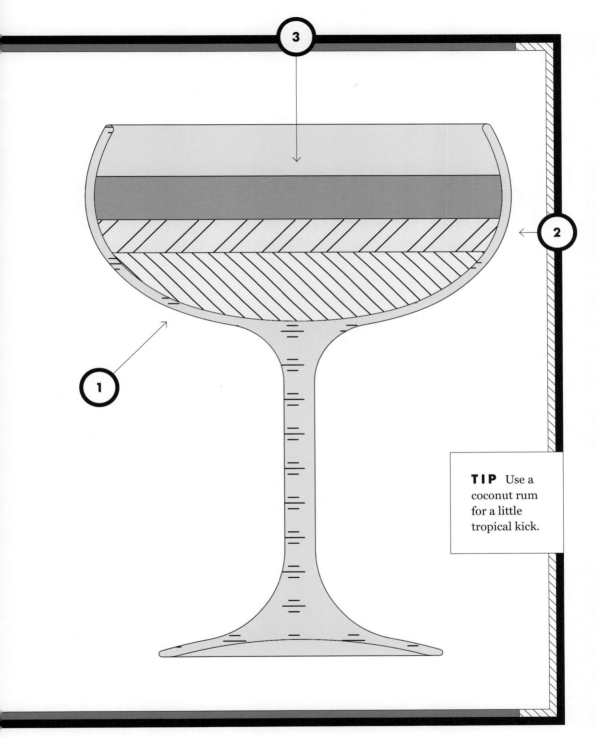

TIP Use a coconut rum for a little tropical kick.

Modern Classics

Rather refined, completely contemporary: these drinks show off your home mixing skills with rare ingredients, from agave and aperitives, to recipes with some serious pear-power.

THE QUEEN MUM

Gin and Dubonnet (the sweet wine-based aperitif) is thought to have been the Queen Mother's favourite tipple, and who are we to disagree? Think of this potent royal cocktail as a sweet Negroni with a fragrant orange blossom bouquet.

INGREDIENTS

1	gin	60 ml (2 oz)
2	Dubonnet	60 ml (2 oz)
3	orange blossom water	dash
4	Angostura bitters	dash
5	orange twist	to garnish

EQUIPMENT

Mixing glass, bar spoon, strainer

METHOD

Add the liquids to a mixing glass and stir with ice, then strain into a glass with a rock of ice. Garnish with a large piece of orange twist.

GLASS TYPE:
TUMBLER
OR COUPE

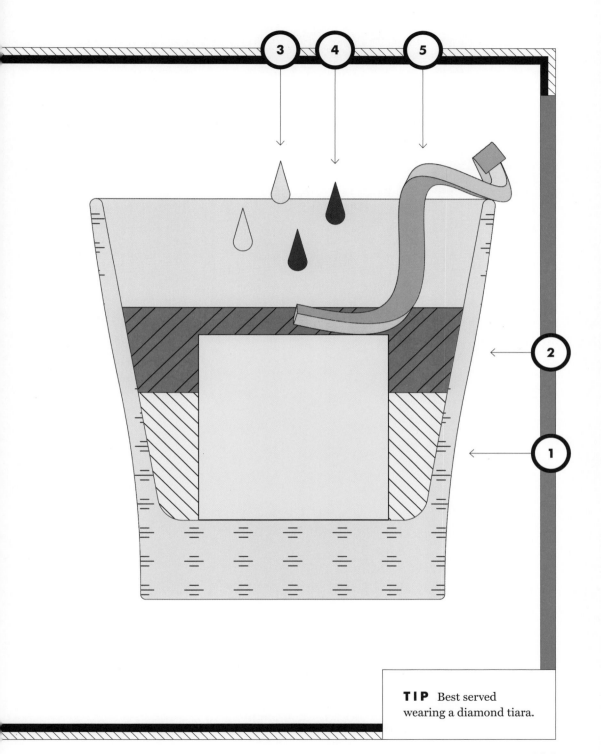

TIP Best served
wearing a diamond tiara.

AMERICAN APERITIF

This simple, bourbon-powered aperitif uses ginger syrup and amaro liqueur for a dry, refreshingly bitter drink, a perfect alternative for those poor unfortunates who have over-imbibed on their summer Negronis.

INGREDIENTS

1	bourbon	60 ml (2 oz)
2	amaro-style liqueur	60 ml (2 oz)
3	ginger syrup	30 ml (1 oz)
4	lemon slice	to garnish

EQUIPMENT

Mixing glass, bar spoon, strainer

METHOD

Add the liquids to a mixing glass with ice, stir and strain into a tumbler over ice. Add lemon slice and serve.

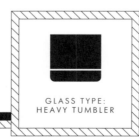

GLASS TYPE:
HEAVY TUMBLER

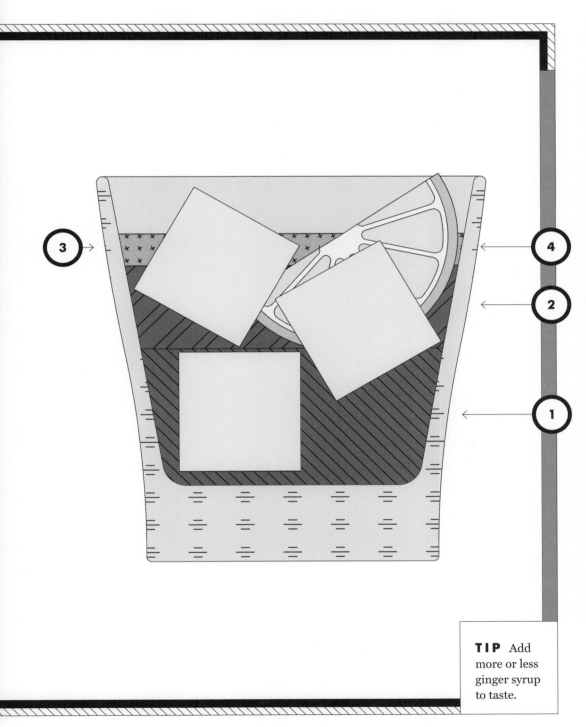

TIP Add more or less ginger syrup to taste.

THE SOUTHSIDE

This prohibition classic is said to have originated at the Twenty-One Club in NYC, inspired by a long version over crushed ice drunk by Chicago mobsters. It's fresh, zingy and slightly illegal-tasting.

INGREDIENTS

1	fresh mint sprigs	2–3
2	gin	60 ml (2 oz)
3	lime juice, freshly squeezed	30 ml (1 oz)
4	Simple Syrup (page 29)	15 ml (½ oz)
5	fresh mint sprig	to garnish

EQUIPMENT

Muddler, shaker, strainer

METHOD

Softly bruise the mint, shake the liquids over ice and strain into a martini glass or coupe. Garnish with a fresh mint sprig.

GLASS TYPE:
COUPE OR MARTINI

TIP Dress like a 1930s mobster before you take your first sip.

NICE PEAR

There's nothing like a nice, ripe pear. This cocktail makes full use of this fact with good quality pear juice, a spicy note of ginger and a top-quality gin.

INGREDIENTS

1	pear juice, freshly squeezed	60 ml (2 oz)
2	premium gin	60 ml (2 oz)
3	Spiced Brown Sugar Syrup (see flavoured syrup method, page 31)	15 ml (½ oz)
4	grated crystallised ginger	to garnish
5	fresh mint sprig	to garnish

EQUIPMENT

Juicer or blender and fine sieve, shaker, strainer

METHOD

Shake the liquids over ice and strain into a coupe. Grate over a little crystallised ginger and add a sprig of mint to garnish.

GLASS TYPE:
COUPE

TIP Add a dash of fresh lime juice if your pear is a little too sweet.

WHISKY GRENADINE

This punch-like recipe leans heavily on grenadine and super-fresh grapefruit for a refreshing, summery sipper that has just the right amount of tartness. Works just as well sloshed into a paper cup at a balcony BBQ as it does delicately poured into a crystal cut rocks glass at your parents' wedding anniversary. You do you.

INGREDIENTS

1	pink grapefruit juice, freshly squeezed	60 ml (2 oz)
2	bourbon or rye	30 ml (1 oz)
3	red (sweet) vermouth	30 ml (1 oz)
4	grenadine	10 ml (⅓ oz)
5	lemon wheel	½, to garnish
6	maraschino cherry	to garnish

EQUIPMENT

Shaker, strainer

METHOD

Shake the liquids over ice until frosty and strain into a tumbler filled with ice. Garnish with a lemon wheel and a cocktail cherry.

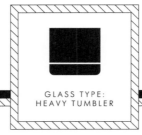

GLASS TYPE:
HEAVY TUMBLER

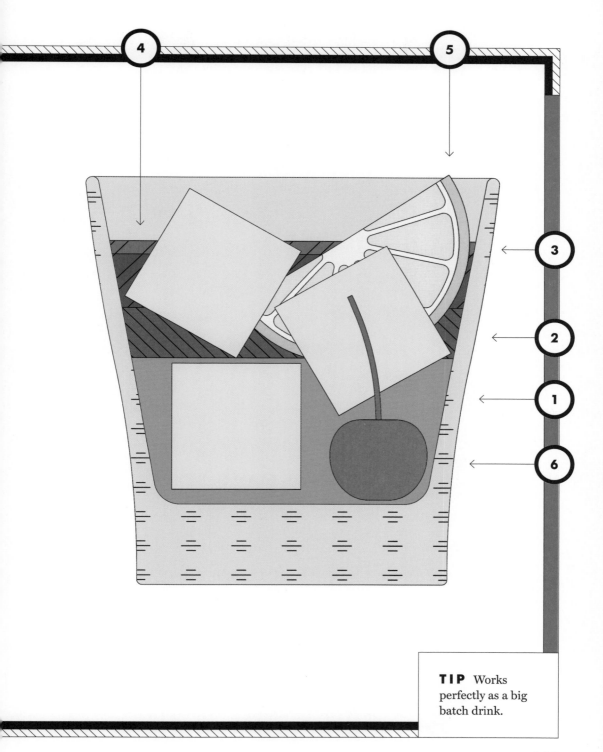

TIP Works perfectly as a big batch drink.

JUAN COLLINS

Power-up a Tom Collins (created in the late 1870s by US cocktail legend, Jerry Thomas) with tequila rather than the classic gin. It's a pared down cocktail designed to reveal the quality of the tequila – so use a classy one.

INGREDIENTS

1	reposado tequila	45 ml (1½ oz)
2	lemon juice, freshly squeezed	30 ml (1 oz)
3	agave syrup	15 ml (½ oz)
4	soda water	60 ml (2 oz)
5	lime wedge	to garnish
6	maraschino cherry	to garnish

EQUIPMENT

Bar spoon

METHOD

Pour the tequila, lemon juice and agave syrup into a glass filled with ice. Stir and top up with soda. Squeeze the lime wedge over the drink and drop into the glass with a maraschino cherry.

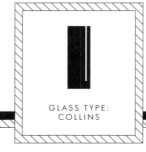

GLASS TYPE:
COLLINS

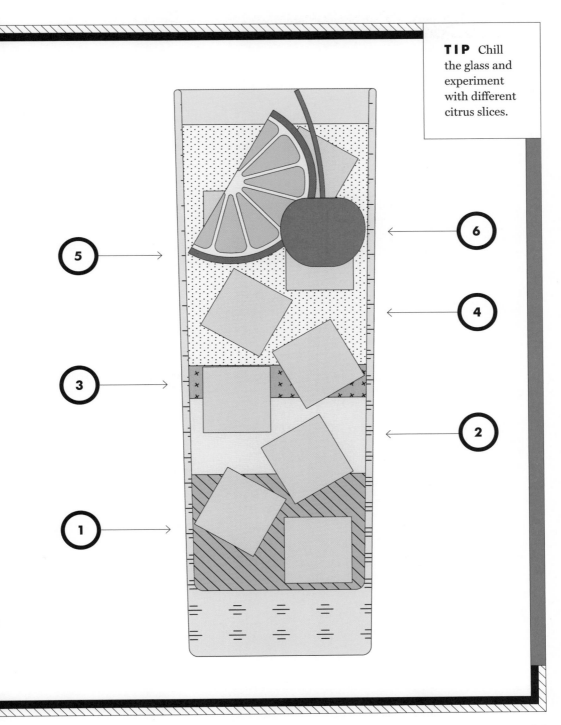

TIP Chill the glass and experiment with different citrus slices.

CEREZADE

Frangipane and jam in a glass. Smooth gold tequila, ruby-toned cherry juice, ripe citrus and a little almond liqueur. Top up with a tart lemonade to keep things sweet, or swap with chilled soda water for a little extra freshness.

INGREDIENTS

1	orange wedge	1
2	lemon wedge	1
3	mezcal	45 ml (1½ oz)
4	cherry juice	30 ml (1 oz)
5	Simple Syrup (page 29)	15 ml (½ oz)
6	almond liqueur	15 ml (½ oz)
7	Angostura bitters	dash
8	clear lemonade	to top up

EQUIPMENT

Muddler, shaker, strainer and bar spoon

METHOD

Muddle the orange and lemon wedges in a shaker, then fill with ice. Add the mezcal, cherry juice, syrup, almond liqueur and a dash of bitters. Shake hard to chill. Strain into a glass filled with ice and top up with clear lemonade. Churn once gently with a bar spoon.

GLASS TYPE:
HIGHBALL OR COLLINS

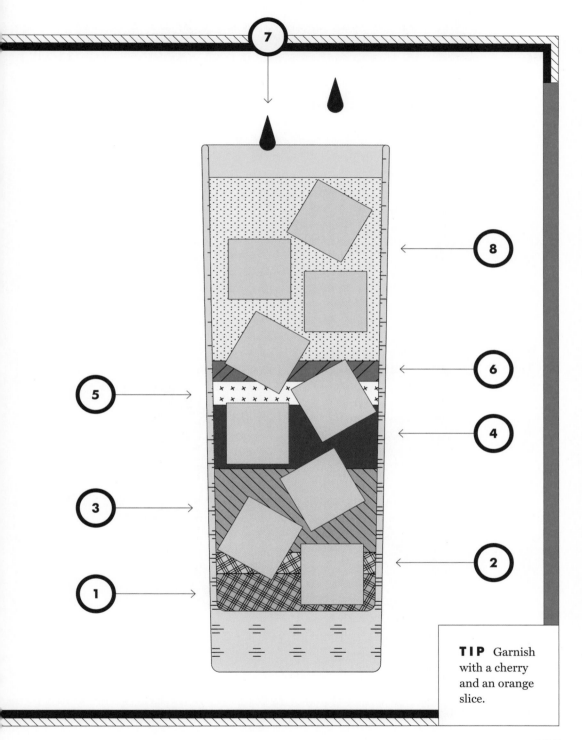

TIP Garnish with a cherry and an orange slice.

AGAVE ICED TEA

Imagine the most delicious cup of tea you've ever tasted. Now, imagine it with tequila, lime and agave syrup. Mind-blowing, right? This twisted iced tea recipe uses gold tequila, gold rum and ginger ale with a little agave sweetness.

INGREDIENTS

1	gold tequila	15 ml (½ oz)
2	vodka	15 ml (½ oz)
3	gold rum	15 ml (½ oz)
4	triple sec	15 ml (½ oz)
5	lime juice, freshly squeezed	15 ml (½ oz)
6	agave syrup	15 ml (½ oz)
7	ginger ale	to top up
8	lime wedge	to garnish

EQUIPMENT

Shaker, strainer

METHOD

Pour the tequila, vodka, rum, triple sec and lime juice into a shaker with ice and shake until frothy and cold. Strain into an ice-filled glass. Top up with ginger ale and garnish with a lime wedge squeezed on top.

GLASS TYPE:
HIGHBALL

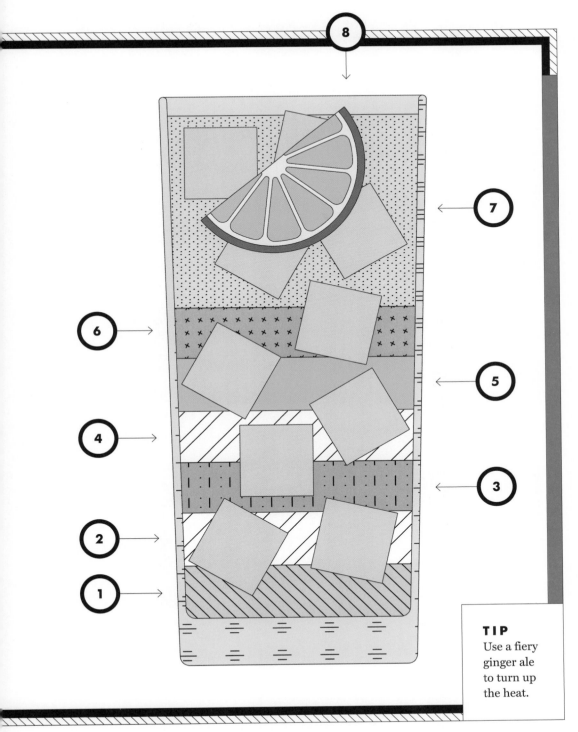

TIP
Use a fiery ginger ale to turn up the heat.

PINK PALOMA

This fresh, zingy drink, topped with chilled soda water, uses mandarin or premium vodka as its base, pepped up with ruby grapefruit and lime. The original Paloma, with tequila and a splash of grapefruit soda, is popular in Spain, but this grown-up vodka version of the Spanish teen fave is just the ticket.

INGREDIENTS

1	mandarin or premium vodka	60 ml (2 oz)
2	ruby grapefruit, freshly squeezed	½ grapefruit
3	lime juice, freshly squeezed	15 ml (½ oz)
4	agave or Simple Syrup (page 29)	15 ml (½ oz)
5	soda water	to top up
6	lime wheel	to garnish

EQUIPMENT

Shaker, strainer

METHOD

Pour the vodka, juices and syrup into an ice-filled shaker. Shake vigorously and strain into an ice-filled glass. Top up with soda and garnish with a lime wheel.

GLASS TYPE:
JAM JAR OR TUMBLER

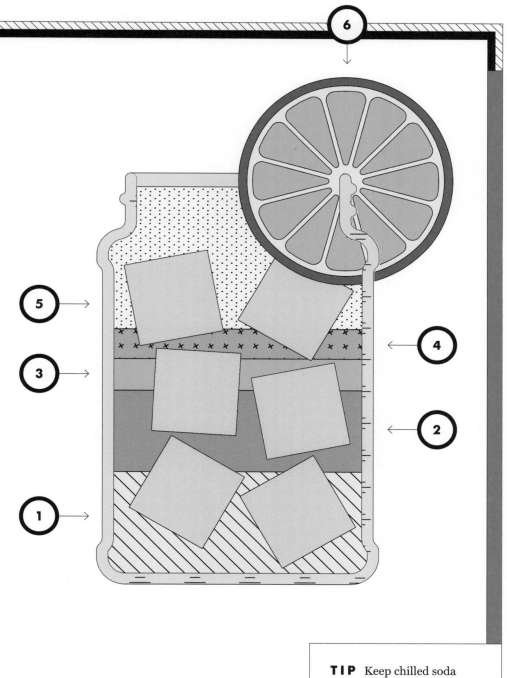

TIP Keep chilled soda water on hand for top-ups.

ULTIMATE VODKA ORANGE

Even the most perfect couple needs to open things up once in a while. Change up the classic pairing of vodka and orange with vanilla tones, freshly squeezed juice and a couple of drops of orange bitters for eye-crossing aromatics. You'll never go back.

INGREDIENTS

1	vanilla vodka	30 ml (1 oz)
2	orange juice, freshly squeezed	to top up
3	orange bitters	2 dashes
4	orange wheel	to garnish

METHOD

Add the vodka to a highball glass or tumbler filled halfway with ice. Top up with the orange juice and bitters. Garnish with an orange wheel.

GLASS TYPE:
HIGHBALL OR
TUMBLER

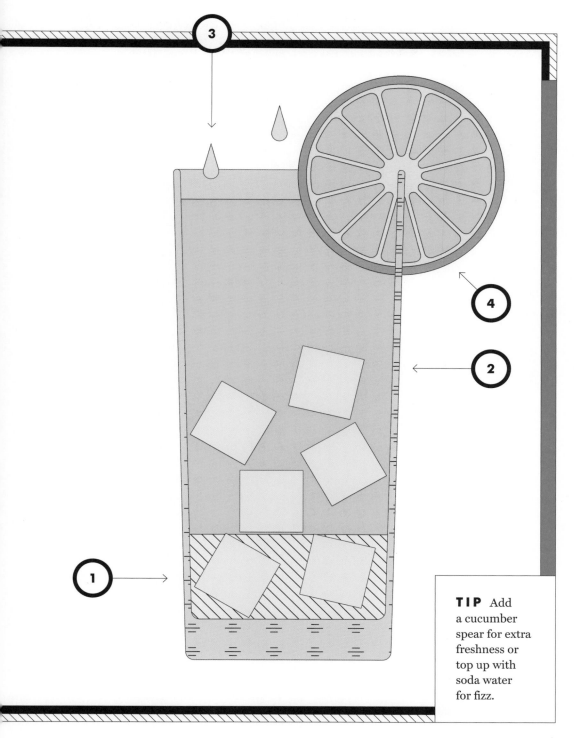

TIP Add a cucumber spear for extra freshness or top up with soda water for fizz.

PINK VODKA LEMONADE

A summer party favourite, Pink Vodka Lemonade is a criminally tasty way to drink vodka. The added lemon juice keeps it tart and the raspberry-infused premium vodka elevates this drink from downgrade party punch to something altogether classier.

INGREDIENTS

1	Absolut Raspberri vodka	30 ml (1 oz)
2	cranberry juice	30 ml (1 oz)
3	lemon juice, freshly squeezed	15 ml (½ oz)
4	chilled lemonade	to top up
5	rhubarb bitters	2 dashes
6	lime wheels	to garnish

METHOD

Add the vodka, cranberry and lemon juices to a highball over ice and top up with lemonade. Add the bitters and garnish with lime wheels.

GLASS TYPE:
HIGHBALL

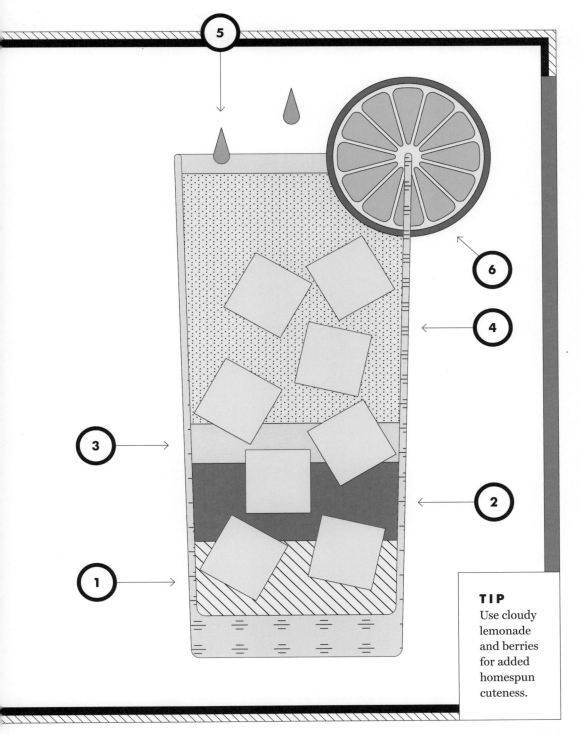

TIP
Use cloudy
lemonade
and berries
for added
homespun
cuteness.

House Party

Magical party-worthy concoctions that can
be made in batches, or with a mindbending twist,
from Backyard Sangria and Coconut Rum Punch
to a rather Thirsty Cowboy.

THE SNOOP (AKA GIN & JUICE)

Back in 1993, Snoop Dogg rapped about Gin & Juice on his debut album *Doggystyle*, and the drink formerly associated with grandmothers everywhere suddenly had its own gangsta swagger. It's potent and the cinnamon adds a little fire. Make sure the citrus juices are freshly squeezed.

INGREDIENTS (SERVES 10–12)

1	lime juice, freshly squeezed	175 ml (6 oz)
2	Cinnamon Syrup (see flavoured syrup method, page 31)	175 ml (6 oz)
3	gin	750 ml (25 oz)
4	cranberry juice	350 ml (12 oz)
5	pineapple juice	350 ml (12 oz)
6	orange juice, freshly squeezed	350 ml (12 oz)
7	orange slices	to garnish
8	lime slices	to garnish
9	pineapple chunks	to garnish

EQUIPMENT

Juicer (hand-held or machine)

METHOD

Add the lime juice, cinnamon syrup and gin to the pitcher and stir well. Add the remaining liquids over large ice cubes. Serve with citrus slices and pineapple chunks to garnish.

GLASS TYPE:
PITCHER
AND PAPER CUPS

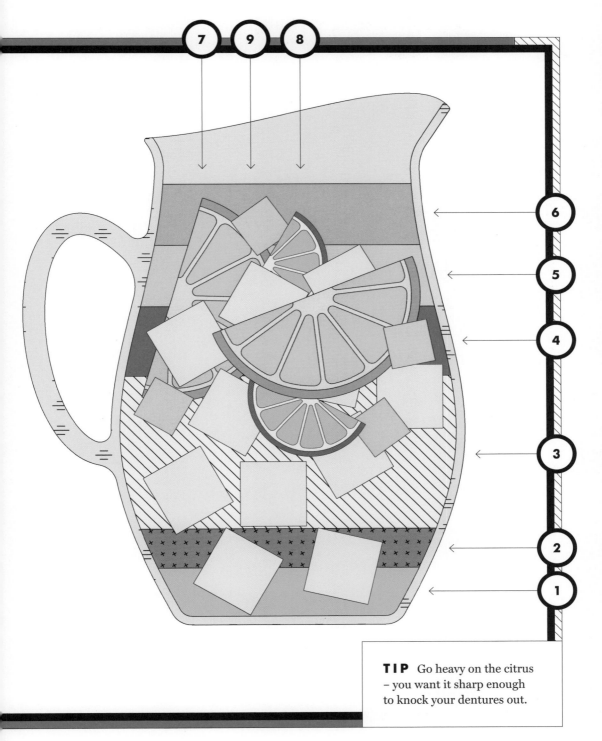

TIP Go heavy on the citrus – you want it sharp enough to knock your dentures out.

HONEY BEER PUNCH

A sweet, beery take on Long Island Iced Tea with gin, honey and a premium brew creating a slip-down punch for one. Add more honey to taste.

INGREDIENTS

1	honey	1 tsp
2	hot water	splash
3	lemon juice, freshly squeezed	15 ml (½ oz)
4	gin	60 ml (2 oz)
5	chilled premium beer	to top up
6	lemon slice	to garnish

EQUIPMENT

Mixing glass, bar spoon

METHOD

Melt a generous teaspoon of honey in a mixing glass with a splash of hot water and allow to cool. Add to a tall glass filled with ice, lemon juice and gin. Stir and top with chilled beer, adding a lemon slice to garnish.

GLASS TYPE:
HIGHBALL

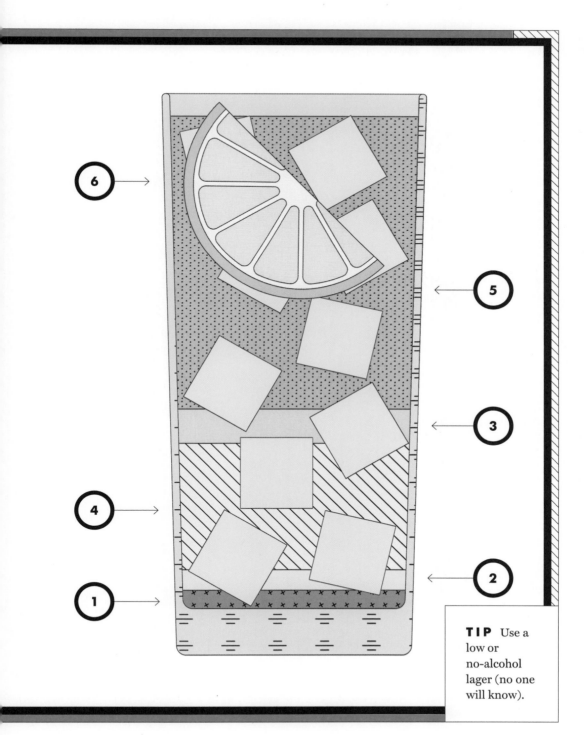

TIP Use a low or no-alcohol lager (no one will know).

BACKYARD SANGRIA

A fragrant, white sangria with a tropical edge that's criminally easy to put together; perfect for backyard summer parties or just-out-of-prison get-togethers. Is your celebration impromptu? Add a few large chunks of ice for quick chilling, or blend all ingredients with a cup of crushed ice for sangria slushies.

INGREDIENTS (SERVES 4–6)

1	orange	½
2	strawberries	4–5
3	pineapple chunks	handful
4	white rum	250 ml (8½ oz)
5	lime juice	1 lime
6	dry white wine	1 bottle
7	pineapple juice, freshly squeezed	250 ml (8½ oz)
8	fresh mint sprigs	handful

EQUIPMENT

Bar spoon

METHOD

Finely slice the orange half and halve the strawberries, then place in a glass jug with the pineapple chunks. Pour over the rum, lime juice, wine and pineapple juice, then leave to chill and infuse for 2–3 hours. Add fresh mint leaves, stir gently and serve.

GLASS TYPE:
GLASS JUG AND
PAPER CUPS

TIP Make sure you use freshly squeezed juice wherever possible, and dial up the lime juice to taste.

COCONUT RUM PUNCH

This pale orange-pink rum punch has an ombré grenadine gradient that's a real crowd pleaser. It's also packed with cherries and citrus slices and powered by coconut rum. Serve wearing a coconut-shell bikini.

INGREDIENTS (SERVES 4)

1	orange, lemon and lime slices	½ of each fruit
2	maraschino cherries	5–6
3	coconut rum	250 ml (8½ oz)
4	orange juice, freshly squeezed	500 ml (17 oz)
5	pineapple juice, freshly squeezed	250 ml (8½ oz)
6	coconut water	250 ml (8½ oz)
7	ginger beer	500 ml (17 oz), or more
8	grenadine	250 ml (8½ oz)

METHOD

Half fill your punch bowl or jug with ice, citrus slices and cherries. Pour over the liquids, topping up with ginger beer and finishing with grenadine – pour this slowly so it collects at the bottom of the drink, giving it a subtle gradient.

GLASS TYPE:
PUNCH BOWL
OR JUG

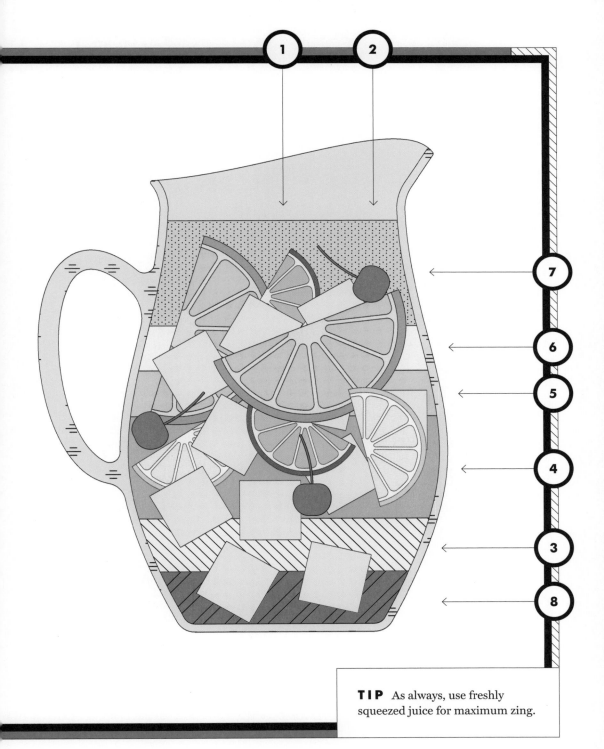

TIP As always, use freshly squeezed juice for maximum zing.

DESERT PUNCH

The delicate, dark-peach colour of this citrus cocktail belies the aged rum and chilli undertone. It has a rich, complex taste that's fresh and zingy with a bright aroma and a tickle of desert heat.

INGREDIENTS

1	chilli	sliver
2	aged rum	60 ml (2 oz)
3	lemon and orange juice mix, freshly squeezed	20 ml (⅔ oz)
4	Simple Syrup (page 29)	10 ml (⅓ oz)
5	orange and mandarin bitters	dash
6	orange twist	to garnish

EQUIPMENT

Muddler, mixing glass or shaker, strainer

METHOD

Muddle the chilli in a mixing glass or shaker, add the liquids and some ice and shake until super frosty. Strain into a chilled glass and garnish with an orange twist.

GLASS TYPE:
COUPE

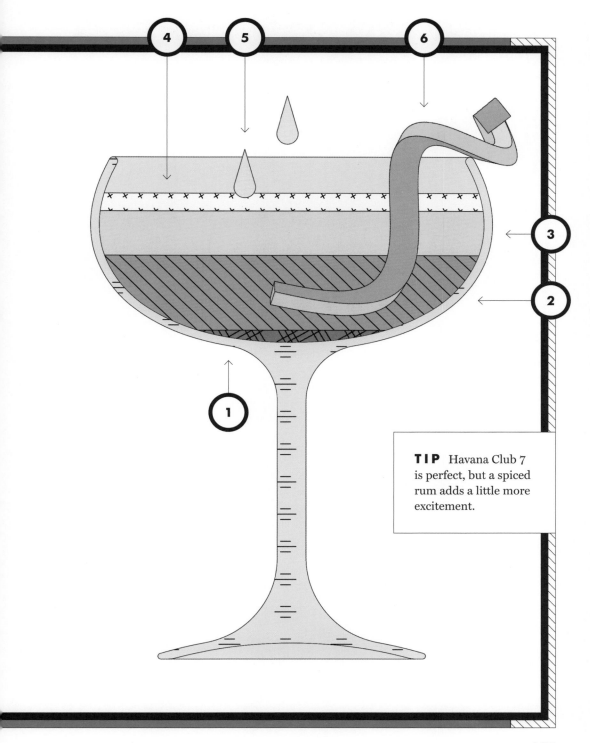

TIP Havana Club 7 is perfect, but a spiced rum adds a little more excitement.

TANGERINE DREAMS

A glut of tangerines bashed into submission, afloat in a lagoon of tequila, Aperol and chilled soda. Delicious, aromatic and moreish. This Aperol Spritz-like punch is the perfect summer party addition.

INGREDIENTS (SERVES 4–6)

1	Aperol	200 ml (7 oz)
2	reposado tequila	200 ml (7 oz)
3	tangerine juice, freshly squeezed	7 tangerines
4	soda water	300 ml (10 oz)
5	tangerine wedges	to garnish

EQUIPMENT

Jug, bar spoon

METHOD

Add the Aperol, tequila and tangerine juice to a large jug filled with ice. Stir the mixture before topping up with soda water and adding the tangerine wedges. Churn gently to combine.

GLASS TYPE:
PUNCH GLASSES OR
TUMBLERS

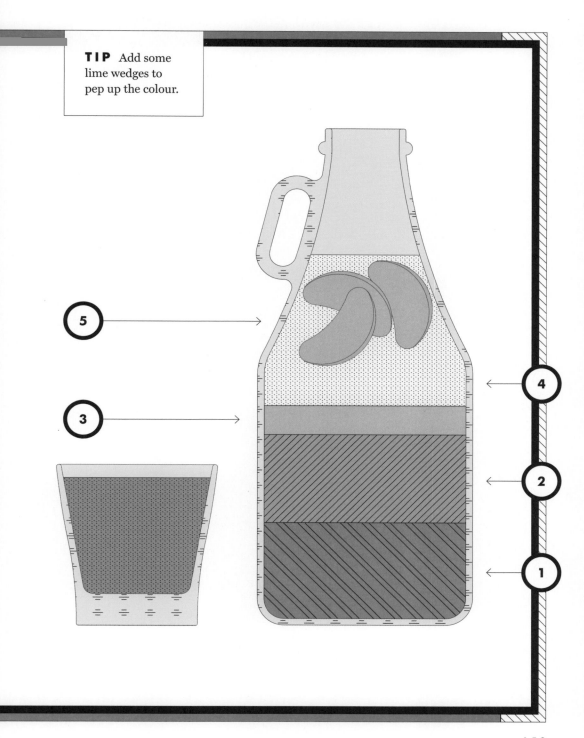

TIP Add some lime wedges to pep up the colour.

5

3

4

2

1

THIRSTY COWBOY

Keep your cowboy well-lubricated with this easy, no-drama bourbon and beer cocktail. Use a dark, musty spirit to give this dude real depth and flavour and your favourite light craft lager rather than a strong ale to keep things firmly in the saddle.

INGREDIENTS

1	bourbon	60ml (2 oz)
2	lemon juice, freshly squeezed	20 ml (⅔ oz)
3	Simple Syrup (page 29)	20 ml (⅔ oz)
4	premium chilled lager	330 ml (11¼ oz)
5	lime twist	to garnish

EQUIPMENT

Shaker, strainer, bar spoon

METHOD

Shake the bourbon, lemon juice and simple syrup over ice until very cold, strain into a pint glass filled with ice, carefully top with beer and slowly stir. Serve with a lime twist.

GLASS TYPE:
PINT

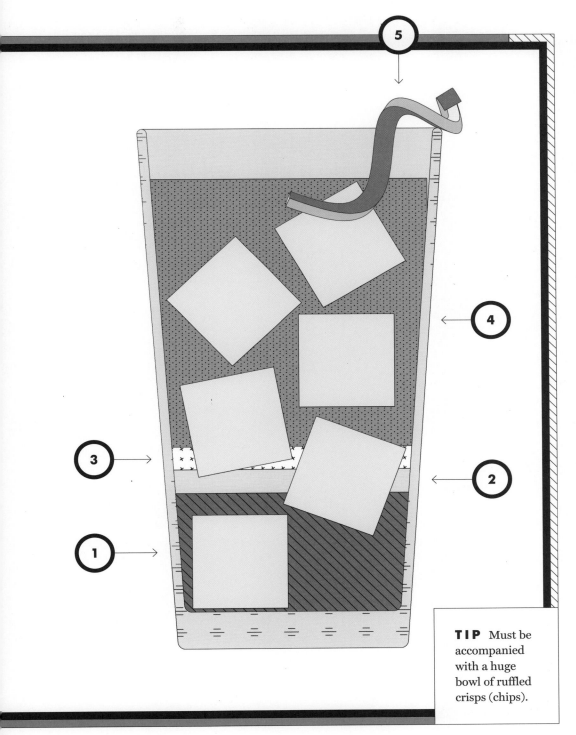

5

4

3

2

1

TIP Must be accompanied with a huge bowl of ruffled crisps (chips).

RUSSIAN SPRING PUNCH

The 1980s in a glass: Russian Spring Punch is up there with the Tequila Sunrise as a drink that embodies a whole decade of classic pop music and dubious haircuts. This highball vodka cocktail is berry-powered with a rather classy Champagne fizz.

INGREDIENTS

1	Absolut Raspberri vodka	30 ml (1 oz)
2	lemon juice, freshly squeezed	30 ml (1 oz)
3	Chambord	10 ml (⅓ oz)
4	agave or Simple Syrup (page 29)	10 ml (⅓ oz)
5	chilled Champagne	to top up
6	mixed berries	to garnish

EQUIPMENT

Shaker, strainer

METHOD

Shake the ingredients (except for the Champagne and berries) vigorously with ice until frosty and strain into a highball over ice. Top up with Champagne and garnish with mixed berries.

GLASS TYPE:
HIGHBALL

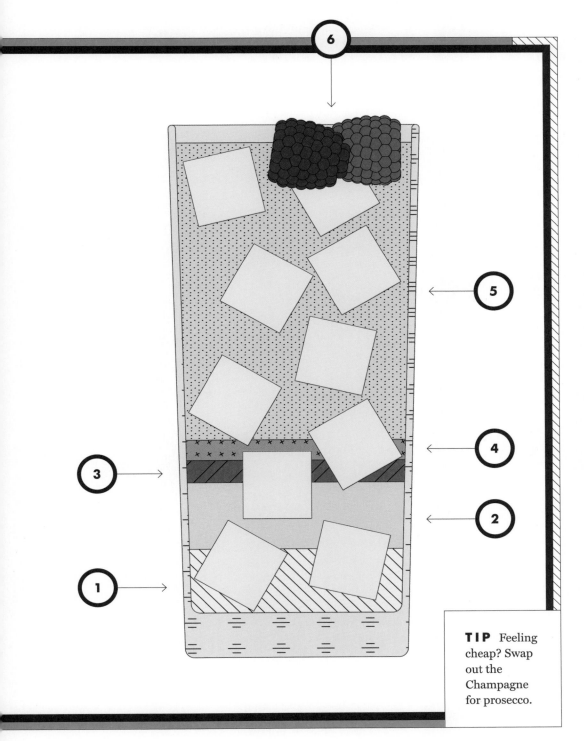

ICED TODDY

Spiced and iced, this cooled-down version of the classic Hot Toddy is delicious.
Jasmine tea lends a floral fragrance, and ginger gives the whole thing a fiery kick.

INGREDIENTS (SERVES 4)

1	lemon and orange zest	6 lemons, 1 orange
2	fresh ginger, peeled and muddled	2–3 slices, plus extra to garnish
3	cloves	5–6
4	cinnamon sticks	3–4
5	lemon juice, freshly squeezed	235 ml (8⅓ oz)
6	orange juice, freshly squeezed	120 ml (4 oz)
7	jasmine teabags	3
8	honey	160 ml (5⅓ oz)
9	whisky	475 ml (15½ oz)
10	orange twists	for serving
11	cardamom or orange bitters	dash, for serving

EQUIPMENT

Jug, fine mesh sieve

METHOD

Peel the orange and lemons leaving the white pith (keep some back for garnishing)
and place in a saucepan with the muddled ginger, spices, citrus juices, teabags and a
cup of water. Bring to the boil, remove from heat and let sit for a few minutes before
removing the teabags and stirring in the honey. Let
cool. Strain through a fine sieve into a jug filled
with two cups of ice and the bourbon. Stir until ice
has melted and serve immediately in toddy glasses
filled with ice, add a couple of drops of bitters, and
garnish with ginger slices.

GLASS TYPE:
HOT TODDY OR
TUMBLER

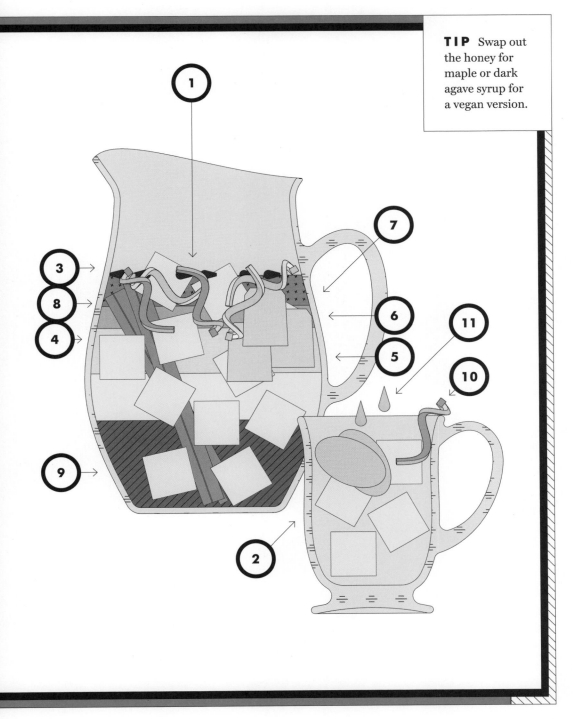

165

Fresh, Long & Plenty of Cucumbers

For those who never want it to end: these delicious punch-like long drinks quench thirst and temper booze's fire power. All that and a cucumber or three.

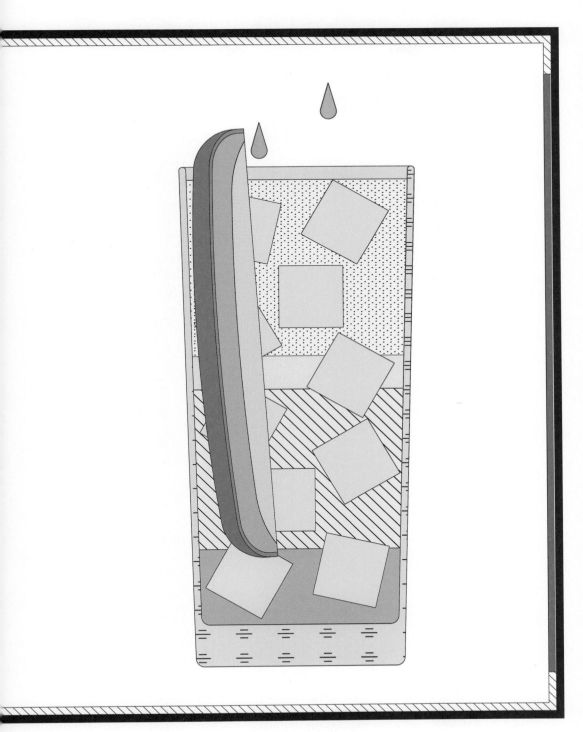

SMASHED CUCUMBER

Cucumber and gin is a perfect combination, and the dill adds a sweet, if not slightly savoury, edge. Swap the dill for fennel tops or celery leaves if you want, but never mess with the cucumber.

INGREDIENTS

1	cucumber juice	30 ml (1 oz)
2	cucumber chunks	handful
3	fresh dill	sprig
4	lime juice, freshly squeezed	15 ml (½ oz)
5	Simple Syrup (page 29)	dash
6	gin	60 ml (2 oz)
7	chilled soda water	to top up
8	cucumber spear	to garnish

EQUIPMENT

Juicer or blender and fine mesh sieve, muddler

METHOD

Juice the cucumber using a juicer (machine) or liquidise and strain through a fine sieve into a glass. Gently muddle a handful of cucumber chunks and the dill with the lime juice and simple syrup. Add the gin, cucumber juice and ice, top with chilled soda water and garnish with a cucumber spear.

GLASS TYPE:
HIGHBALL

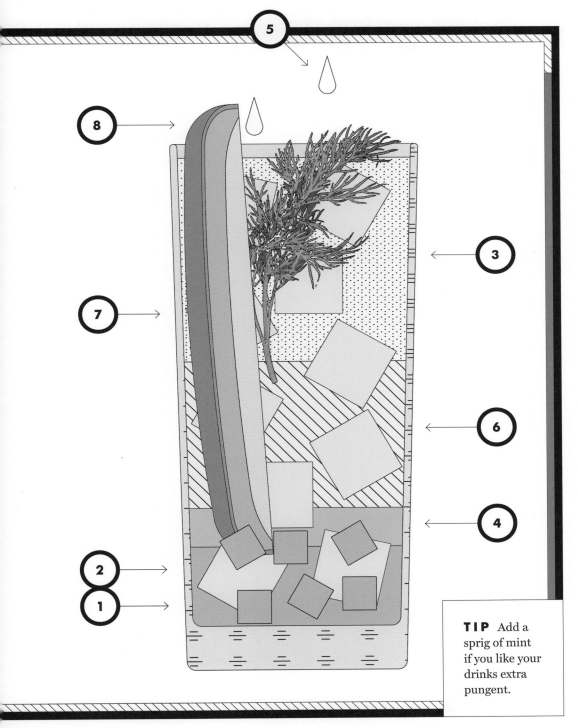

TIP Add a sprig of mint if you like your drinks extra pungent.

CUCUMBER LEMONADE

Imagine making a fresh, zingy and wholesome lemonade of the type seen at kids' lemonade stands across the world, with a sneaky shot of mum and dad's gin thrown in – and all the adults get smashed. And then something happens with a cucumber. That's this drink.

INGREDIENTS

1	cucumber juice	30 ml (1 oz)
2	gin	60 ml (2 oz)
3	lemon juice, freshly squeezed	15 ml (½ oz)
4	agave syrup or Simple Syrup (page 29)	dash
5	cucumber spear	to garnish
6	chilled soda water	to top up

EQUIPMENT

Juicer or blender and fine mesh sieve, shaker, strainer

METHOD

Juice the cucumber using a juicer (machine) or liquidise and strain through a fine mesh sieve. Shake the gin, cucumber and lemon juices, and syrup over ice. Add a cucumber spear and ice cubes to a highball glass, strain the drink into the glass. Top with chilled soda water.

GLASS TYPE:
HIGHBALL

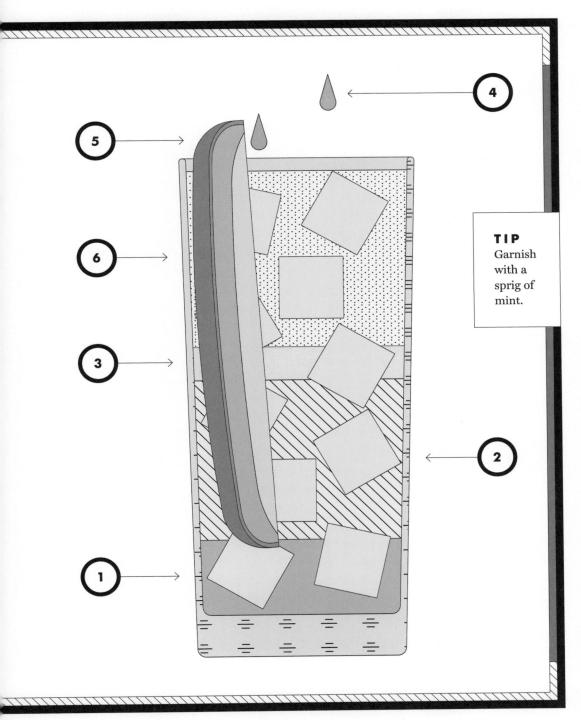

TIP
Garnish with a sprig of mint.

PINE TIP SODA

This woodsy, pine-tip infused sweet soda is a delicious long drink. Make your own Pine Tip Syrup (page 31) using bright green, new pine tips and let it add a manly, live-in-a-log-cabin vibe to your cocktails. Pine syrup works best in a simple, pared-down recipe, but you can always add a little ginger slice if you're the fancy sort.

INGREDIENTS

1	premium vodka	60 ml (2 oz)
2	Pine Tip Syrup (see flavoured syrup method, page 31)	30 ml (1 oz)
3	lemon juice, freshly squeezed	15 ml (½ oz)
4	chilled soda water	to top up

EQUIPMENT

Shaker, strainer

METHOD

Shake the vodka, syrup and lemon juice over ice until frosty and strain into a coupe. Top up with soda water.

GLASS TYPE:
COUPE

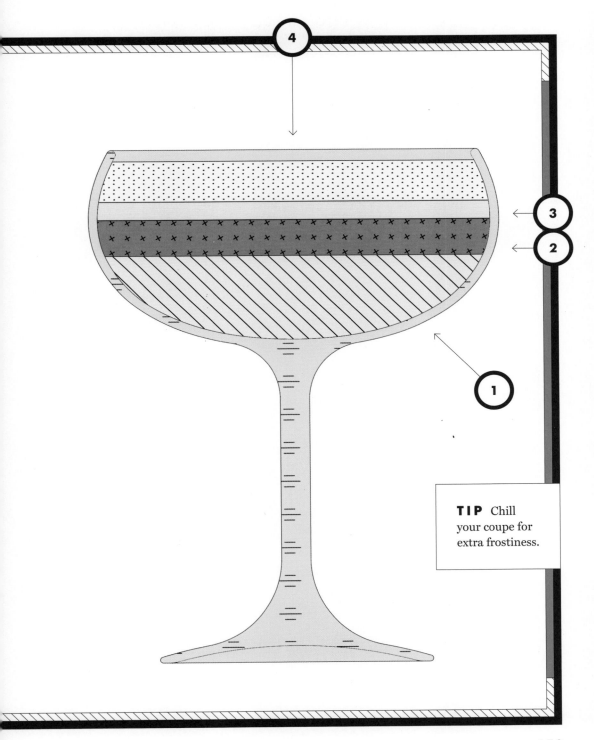

TIP Chill your coupe for extra frostiness.

PERFECT GIN & TONIC

The most perfect drink in the world. Each gin lover has their own way of making this classic cocktail – but the secret is to keep it simple. Oh, and dial up the citrus aroma with fresh lime juice and a drop or two of orange bitters.

INGREDIENTS

1	gin	60 ml (2 oz)
2	lime juice, freshly squeezed	splash
3	cucumber spear	to garnish
4	premium tonic water	to top up
5	orange bitters	dash

METHOD

Add the gin, lime juice and cucumber spear to a highball filled with ice cubes. Top with chilled premium tonic and add a dash of orange bitters.

GLASS TYPE:
HIGHBALL

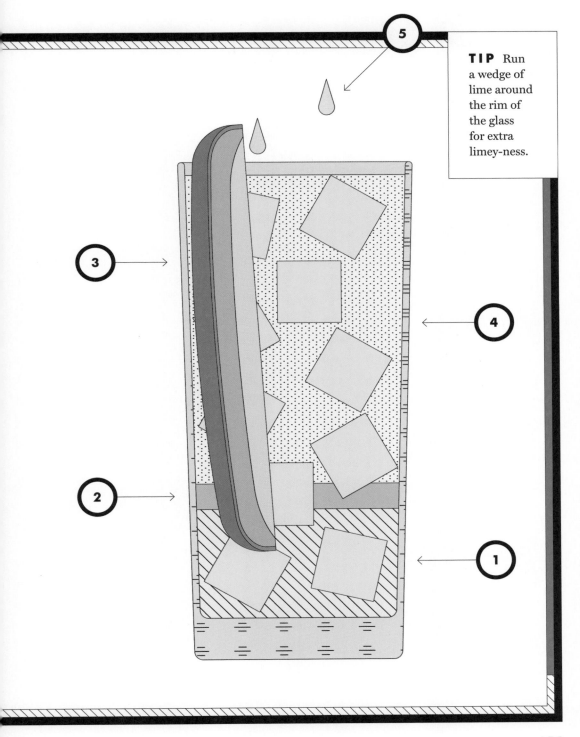

TIP Run a wedge of lime around the rim of the glass for extra limey-ness.

CHIMAYÓ

This classic autumnal cocktail, created by chef Arturo Jaramillo in the 1960s, was inspired by the small, sweet, red chimayó apples of New Mexico. It's a simple recipe – deliciously sweet – and packs a kick.

INGREDIENTS

1	gold tequila	45 ml (1½ oz)
2	lemon juice, freshly squeezed	15 ml (½ oz)
3	crème de cassis	7.5 ml (¼ oz)
4	cloudy apple juice	90 ml (3 oz)
5	apple slices	to garnish

EQUIPMENT

Bar spoon

METHOD

Pour all of the liquids into a glass half-filled with ice, stir and garnish with the apple slices.

GLASS TYPE:
HIGHBALL

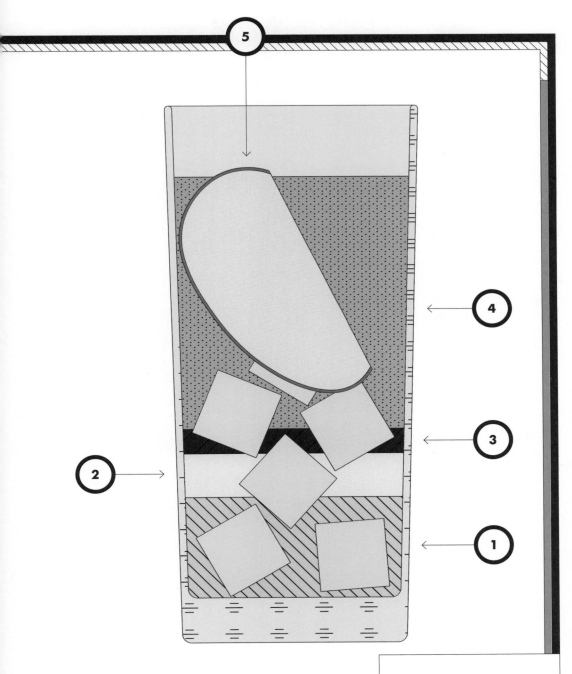

TIP Serve on the rocks, straight up, or as a punch.

PINK GIN SPRITZ

For those who hanker for a Negroni at breakfast – but are embarrassed it looks a bit serious for 7.45 am. This delightfully rose-hued cocktail is topped with chilled pink grapefruit juice to mask your sins.

INGREDIENTS

1	gin	60 ml (2 oz)
2	Aperol	30 ml (1 oz)
3	Campari	15 ml (½ oz)
4	Spiced Brown Sugar Syrup (see flavoured syrup method, page 31)	dash
5	chilled pink grapefruit juice	to top up

EQUIPMENT

Shaker

METHOD

Shake the gin, Aperol, Campari and brown sugar syrup over ice. Add to a Champagne flute and top with the chilled pink grapefruit juice.

GLASS TYPE:
CHAMPAGNE
FLUTE

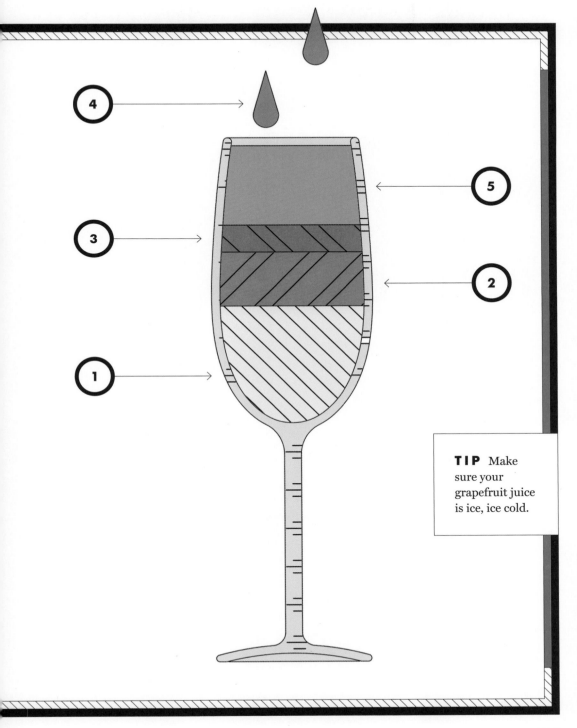

TIP Make sure your grapefruit juice is ice, ice cold.

TIGER'S BLOOD

A variation of the classic daiquiri – just as fresh and bright, but with a dark, spiced kick and blood-red tone. Use fresh pomegranate juice if possible (blend the seeds, not the pith, then sieve); your home bar area will end up blood-splattered like a crime scene, but it's worth it.

INGREDIENTS

1	white rum	60 ml (2 oz)
2	lime juice, freshly squeezed	30 ml (1 oz)
3	pomegranate juice, fresh if possible	15 ml (½ oz)
4	Star Anise and Chilli syrup (see flavoured syrup method, page 31)	15 ml (½ oz)
5	pomegranate seeds	to garnish

EQUIPMENT

Shaker and strainer, blender and fine mesh sieve

METHOD

Fill a shaker with crushed ice, add the rum, lime juice, pomegranate juice, and star anise and chilli syrup, then shake with all your might until frothy. Strain into a chilled glass and garnish with pomegranate seeds. Alternatively, add the ice and all the liquids to a blender and whizz.

GLASS TYPE:
COUPE

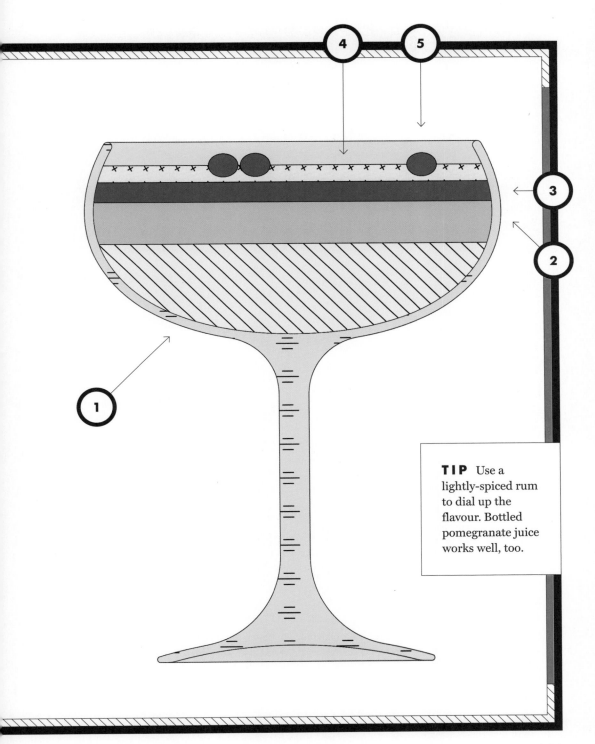

TIP Use a lightly-spiced rum to dial up the flavour. Bottled pomegranate juice works well, too.

ICED WATERMELON FIZZ

Imagine a chilled watermelon blended into an icy-fresh, slushie-style cocktail that's packed with booze. The Watermelon Fizz is a blended cocktail topped up with tonic water for extra sharpness. Serve with tequila-laced watermelon slices, because why not?

INGREDIENTS

1	silver tequila	45 ml (1½ oz)
2	lime juice, freshly squeezed	15 ml (½ oz)
3	triple sec	15 ml (½ oz)
4	agave syrup	15 ml (½ oz)
5	peeled watermelon chunks	handful
6	tonic water	to top up
7	watermelon slice	to garnish

EQUIPMENT

Blender

METHOD

Blend the ingredients (except the tonic and garnish) with a small scoop of crushed ice until slushy. Pour into a glass and top up with tonic. Garnish with a slice of watermelon.

GLASS TYPE:
HIGHBALL

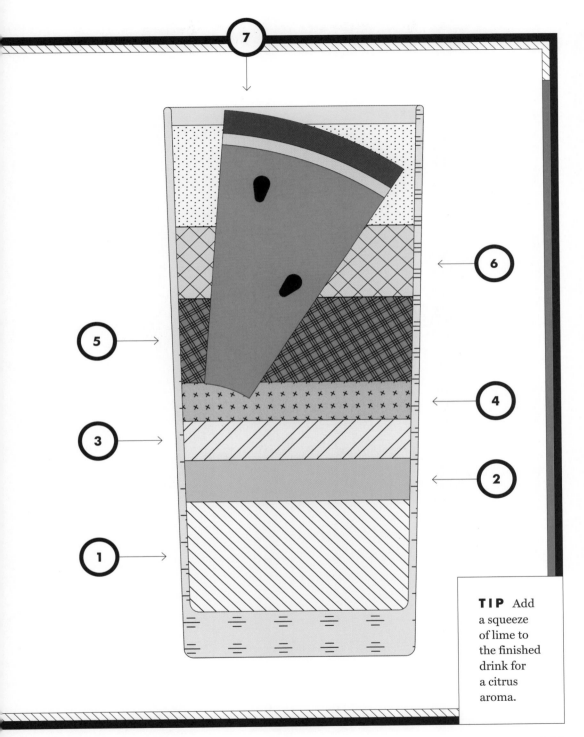

Tropical & Tiki

It's time to unleash your coconuts. Is there any taste combo more tropical than rum and nature's tastiest nut? Standby for the eyepopping Piña Ombré, two perfect daiquiris, and more.

PIÑA OMBRÉ

A tiki-inspired barn-stormer with coconut sorbet and a Pinterest-worthy ombré gradient. This fresh, creamy, frozen-dessert-like cocktail is 100 per cent easy on the eye: like an edible deluxe spray tan with ab-contouring and a shimmer finish. Note: this recipe makes two drinks, or one giant one for a solo night in.

INGREDIENTS (SERVES 1–2)

1	coconut rum	90 ml (3 oz)
2	coconut sorbet	1 scoop
3	coconut or almond milk	250 ml (8½ oz)
4	frozen pineapple chunks	250 ml (8½ oz)
5	grenadine	2 dashes

EQUIPMENT

Blender

METHOD

Add half the rum, all of the coconut sorbet and the coconut or almond milk to a blender with a handful of ice cubes, whizz and set aside. Then add the remaining rum to the blender with the frozen pineapple and whizz. Pour half out and set aside, then add a dash of grenadine to the remaining mixture and whizz briefly. Add a dash of grenadine to the glass (or glasses), followed by the pink pineapple mixture, then the yellow, until the glass is half full. Top with the white mixture.

GLASS TYPE:
TUMBLER

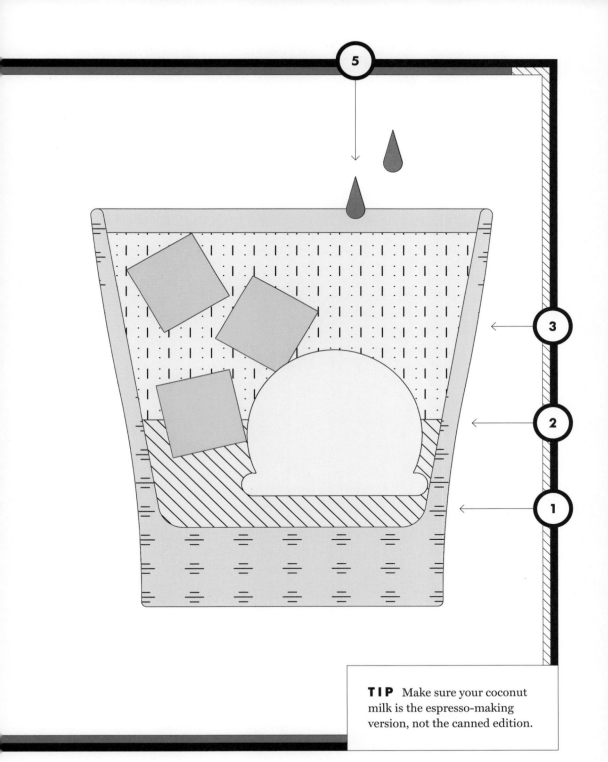

TIP Make sure your coconut milk is the espresso-making version, not the canned edition.

BANANAS FOSTER

The iconic, retro, flambéed banana dessert – popular in the 1980s – reworked as a frozen, blended rum cocktail with added honeycomb. This recipe is foolproof, but requires the potential embarrassment of purchasing a bottle of banana liqueur (perhaps ask a friend to buy it for you). Otherwise, delicious.

INGREDIENTS

1	dark spiced rum	60 ml (2 oz)
2	banana liqueur	25 ml (¾ oz)
3	medium banana	1
4	premium vanilla ice cream	2 scoops
5	almond milk, if desired	splash
6	honeycomb	1 chunk (the size of a small banana), crumbled

EQUIPMENT

Blender

METHOD

Put the rum, banana liqueur, banana and ice cream in a blender with a few ice cubes, adding a splash of almond milk to achieve a lighter, thinner cocktail. Add some of the crumbled honeycomb and whizz once to mix. Serve in a highball glass with crumbled honeycomb on top.

GLASS TYPE:
HIGHBALL

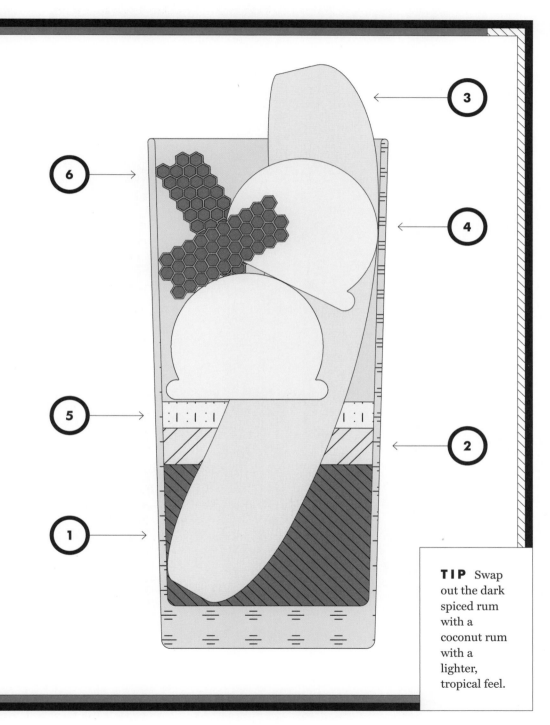

TIP Swap out the dark spiced rum with a coconut rum with a lighter, tropical feel.

PIÑA COLADA

Remember that teenage summer beach holiday when a lithe surfer rubbed coconut suntan oil onto your pudgy limbs – and your heart skipped a beat? This is that feeling, in a glass, with the added tropical power-punch of fresh pineapple and at least three cocktail umbrellas.

INGREDIENTS

1	pineapple chunks	handful
2	white rum	60 ml (2 oz)
3	pineapple juice, freshly squeezed	60 ml (2 oz)
4	coconut cream	60 ml (2 oz)
5	Simple Syrup (page 29)	dash
6	pineapple slice	to garnish

EQUIPMENT

Juice (machine) or blender and fine mesh sieve

METHOD

Juice the pineapple using a juicer (machine) or liquidise with a little water and strain through a fine mesh sieve. Put the pineapple chunks and lots of ice into a blender. Pour over the rum, pineapple juice and coconut cream, add a dash of syrup, and whizz it up until smooth. Serve in a chilled glass (the classic choice is a hurricane, but a coupe or tumbler also works) with a straw, top with a pineapple slice and as many cocktail umbrellas and plastic monkeys as you can muster.

GLASS TYPE: HURRICANE,
COUPE OR TUMBLER

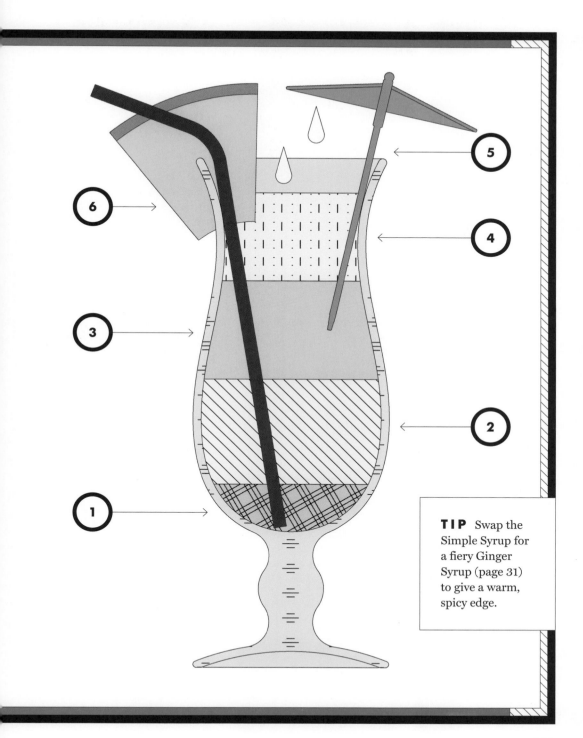

TIP Swap the Simple Syrup for a fiery Ginger Syrup (page 31) to give a warm, spicy edge.

CLASSIC STRAWBERRY DAIQUIRI

Adored by honeymooners, Valentine's-Day daters and drag queens, the deliciously camp Strawberry Daiquiri is an essential cocktail to master. The good news is that it's one of the easiest to make – just be sure your strawberries are plump, ripe and sweet, and your show tunes are at full volume.

INGREDIENTS

1	strawberries	3–4
2	white rum	60 ml (2 oz)
3	lime juice, freshly squeezed	30 ml (1 oz)
4	Simple Syrup (page 29)	15 ml (½ oz)
5	strawberry slice	to garnish

EQUIPMENT

Muddler, mixing glass and shaker, or blender

METHOD

Muddle the strawberries in a mixing glass. Fill a shaker with crushed ice, add the strawberries, rum, lime juice and simple syrup and shake with all your might until frothy. Strain into a chilled glass and garnish with a slice of strawberry. Alternatively, add the ice and ingredients to a blender and whizz for a frozen version.

GLASS TYPE:
COUPE OR MARTINI

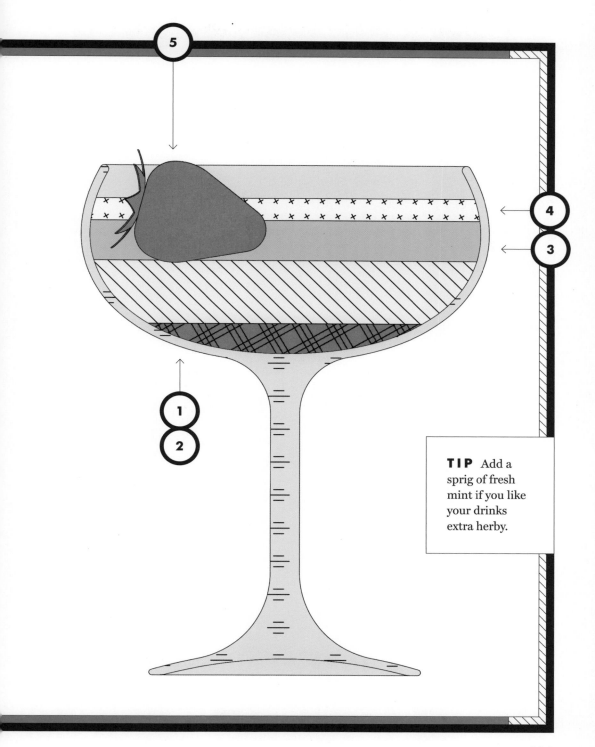

TIP Add a sprig of fresh mint if you like your drinks extra herby.

MAI TAI

The ultimate tiki cocktail, reputed to be the creation of Victor J. Bergeron and the shining star of his fabled 1940s tropical tiki movement that had its beginnings at his famous restaurant and hang-out spot, Trader Vic's. Maita'i is the Tahitian phrase for 'good'. And who are we to argue? Note: orgeat (pronounced or-zsa) is a rich almond syrup and gives the Mai Tai its pleasingly nutty flavour.

INGREDIENTS

1	aged rum	60 ml (2 oz)
2	lime juice, freshly squeezed	25 ml (¾ oz)
3	orange curaçao	15 ml (½ oz)
4	Simple Syrup (page 29)	10 ml (⅓ oz)
5	orgeat syrup	10 ml (⅓ oz)
6	mint sprig	to garnish
7	lime wedge	to garnish

EQUIPMENT

Shaker

METHOD

Shake the liquids over ice until frosty. Serve in a chilled coupe or tumbler, garnish with a mint sprig and lime wedge.

GLASS TYPE:
TUMBLER
OR COUPE

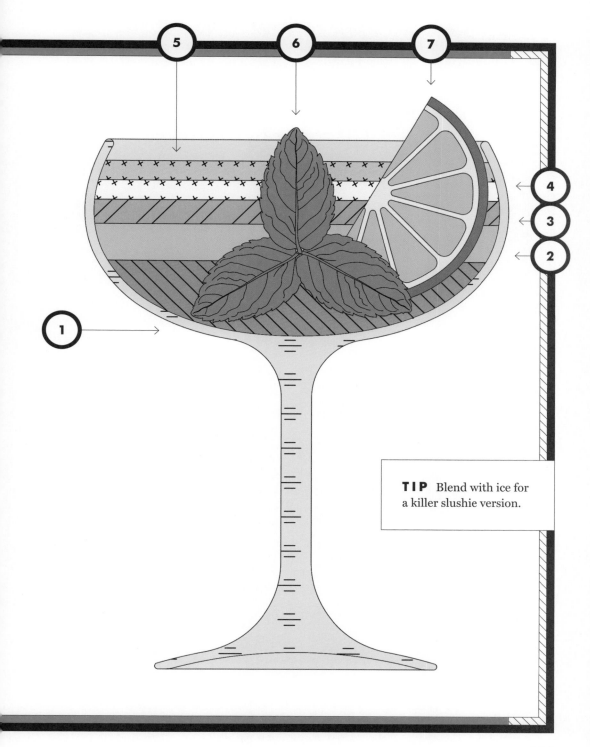

TIP Blend with ice for a killer slushie version.

CHERRY THYME DAIQUIRI

A herby, fragrant and ruby-red concoction that has all the fresh zinginess of the classic daiquiri, and is with an added dark-cherry sweetness that balances perfectly with the sharp citrus notes, lifted by the aroma of fresh thyme. Like being ravished in an overgrown cherry orchard.

INGREDIENTS

1	white rum	60 ml (2 oz)
2	lime juice, freshly squeezed	15 ml (½ oz)
3	Cherry Heering	30 ml (1 oz)
4	Simple Syrup (page 29)	10 ml (⅓ oz)
5	fresh thyme	2 sprigs

EQUIPMENT

Shaker and strainer, or blender

METHOD

Fill a shaker with crushed ice, add the rum, lime juice, Cherry Heering and simple syrup, plus a thyme sprig (rolled between your palms to release the flavour), and shake with all your might until frothy. Strain into a chilled glass, serve with a straw and garnish with another fresh thyme sprig. Alternatively, add the ice and ingredients (pick off some thyme leaves; don't add the stalk) to a blender and whizz.

GLASS TYPE:
HURRICANE

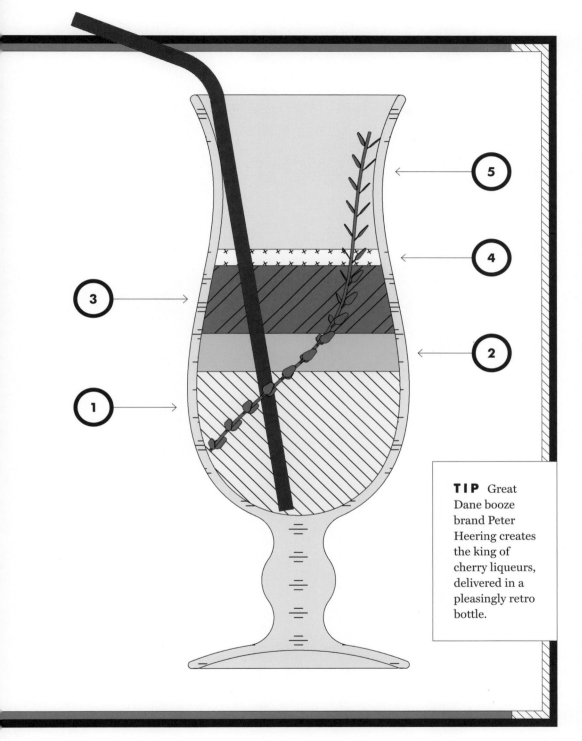

197

Drink the Seasons

Drink seasonally with super-fresh sippers in spring and summer through to berry- and spice-infused concoctions for the colder months.

BEACH HOUSE

This Barbadian classic is covertly tropical. It has the appearance of a simple G & T, but with coconut water instead of tonic. Fresh and sweet, this little number tastes deceptively alcohol-light.

INGREDIENTS

1	gin	60 ml (2 oz)
2	lime juice, freshly squeezed	15 ml (½ oz)
3	chilled coconut water	to top up
4	lime slice	to garnish

EQUIPMENT

Swizzle stick

METHOD

Pour the gin and lime juice into a highball glass over crushed ice, top with coconut water and add a swizzle stick and lime slice to garnish.

GLASS TYPE:
HIGHBALL

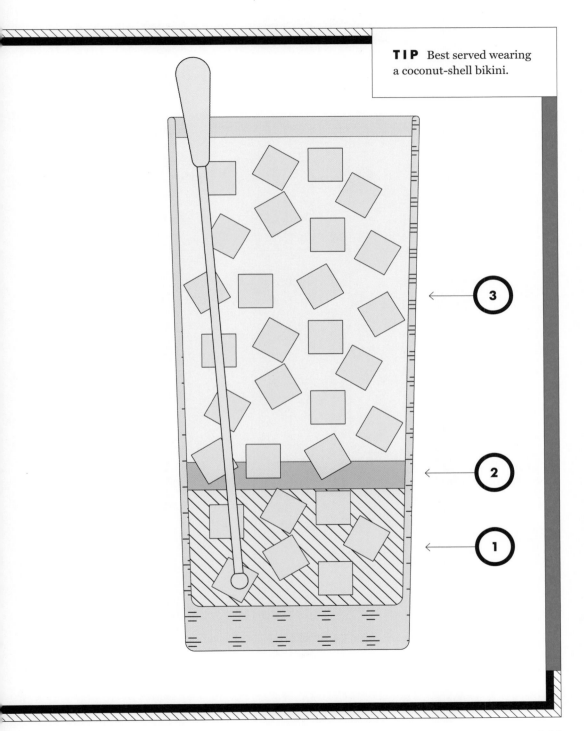

TIP Best served wearing a coconut-shell bikini.

BOURBON SMASH

This simple, refreshing little recipe works well with gin, vodka, tequila and rum, but it's best with a rich, golden bourbon. Remember, this is a recipe that requires a slow hand. Heavy handed muddlers need not apply.

INGREDIENTS

1	mint leaves	5–6
2	bourbon or rye	60 ml (2 oz)
3	Simple Syrup (page 29)	10 ml (⅓ oz)
4	lemon	½, cut lengthways
5	Angostura bitters	dash

EQUIPMENT

Muddler, mixing glass, strainer

METHOD

Gently muddle the mint leaves, lemon, simple syrup in a mixing glass. Add bourbon and then strain into a chilled tumbler, adding crushed ice, then the bitters, and garnishing with mint.

GLASS TYPE:
HEAVY TUMBLER

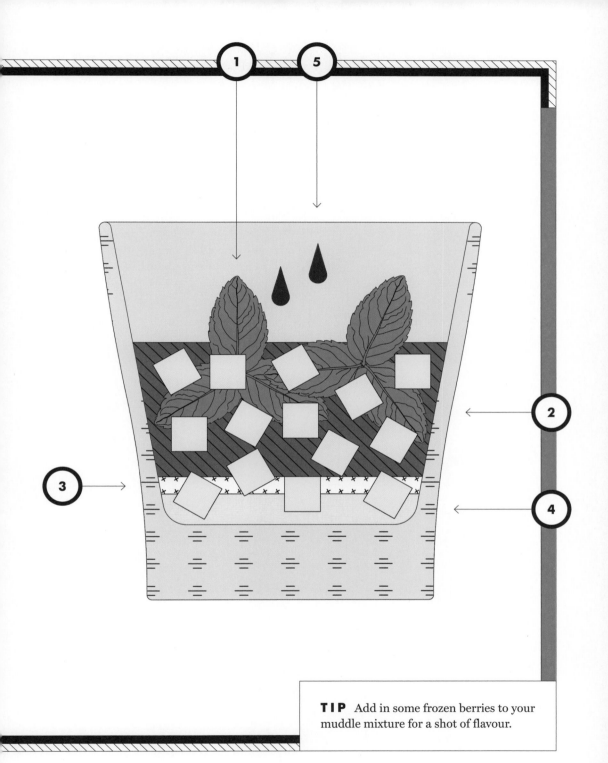

TIP Add in some frozen berries to your muddle mixture for a shot of flavour.

THE LARGERITA

Great things are created when two delicious things are merged into one. The Largerita has a classic Margie base, but it's topped with a smooth, sparkling beer. Perfect for backyard BBQs.

INGREDIENTS

1	mezcal	60 ml (2 oz)
2	orange liqueur	27.5 ml (¾ oz)
3	lime juice, freshly squeezed	30 ml (1 oz)
4	Mexican beer	120 ml (4 oz)
5	lime wheel	to garnish

EQUIPMENT

Shaker, strainer

METHOD

Add the mezcal, orange liqueur and lime juice to a shaker filled with ice. Shake vigorously until the tin is frosty, strain into a chilled glass and top up with beer. Garnish with a lime wheel.

GLASS TYPE:
HIGHBALL

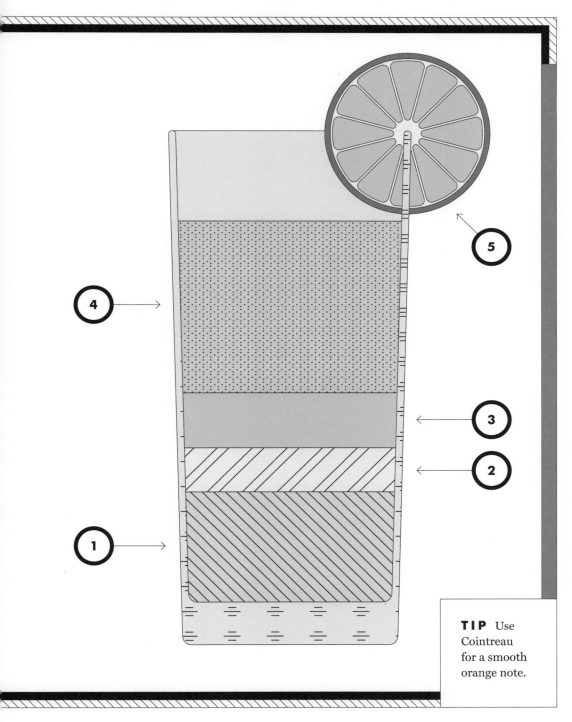

TIP Use Cointreau for a smooth orange note.

FROZEN MANGO MARGIE

Your mangoes need to be perfectly ripe, squishy and aromatic for this recipe to be at its best. Mango and tequila are perfect bedfellows, and the pinch of sea salt intensifies the flavour.

INGREDIENTS

1	silver tequila	30 ml (1 oz)
2	mango, peeled	½
3	lime juice, freshly squeezed	30 ml (1 oz)
4	triple sec	15 ml (½ oz)
5	agave syrup	15 ml (½ oz)
6	sea salt	pinch
7	chilli flakes	pinch
8	lime wedge	to garnish

EQUIPMENT

Blender

METHOD

Place all of the ingredients (except the chilli flakes and garnish) into a blender with a scoop of crushed ice and blend until smooth. Pour into a glass and very lightly sprinkle with chilli flakes. Garnish with a lime wedge.

GLASS TYPE:
MARGARITA OR
LARGE WINE

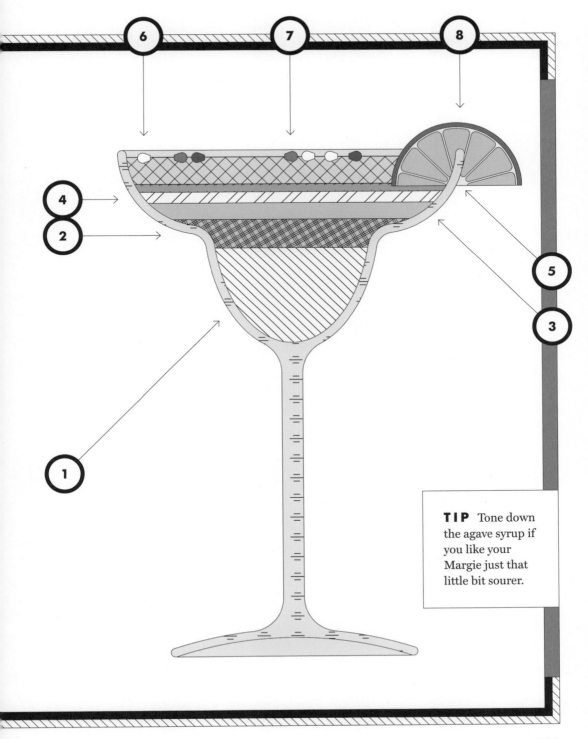

TIP Tone down the agave syrup if you like your Margie just that little bit sourer.

POMEGRANATE SOUR

Pomegranate makes a naturally complex, slightly tart base for this fragrant, tasty recipe. Equal parts premium vanilla vodka and pomegranate juice, plus freshly squeezed lime juice and a dash of ginger syrup, make for a jewel-bright, fruity sipper.

INGREDIENTS

1	vanilla vodka	30 ml (1 oz)
2	pomegranate juice	30 ml (1 oz)
3	lime juice, freshly squeezed	15 ml (½ oz)
4	Ginger Syrup (see flavoured syrup method, page 31)	15 ml (½ oz)
5	pomegranate seeds	to garnish

EQUIPMENT

Shaker, strainer

METHOD

Shake the liquids vigorously over ice until frosty and strain into a martini glass or coupe. Garnish with pomegranate seeds.

GLASS TYPE: MARTINI
OR COUPE

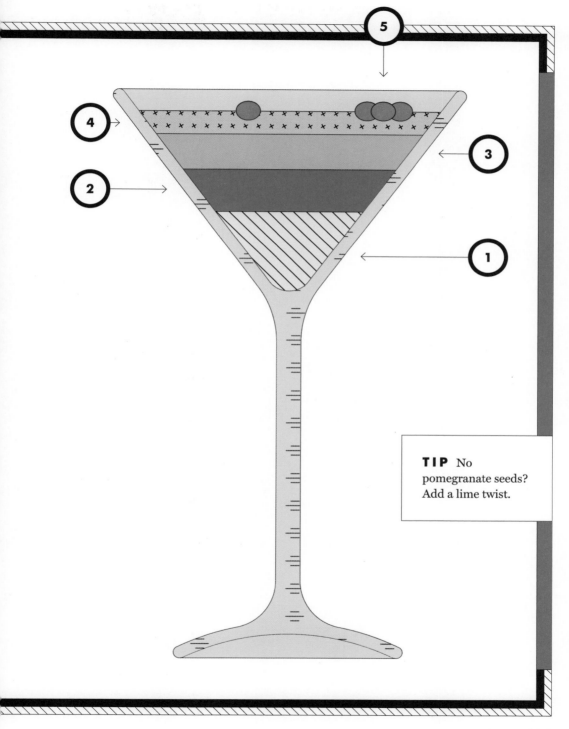

TIP No pomegranate seeds? Add a lime twist.

APPLETINI

This fresh-tasting Apple Martini straddles the sweet/sour divide with perfect balance. Use a good-quality cloudy apple juice or a clear one for a less homespun-looking drink.

INGREDIENTS

1	premium vodka	60 ml (2 oz)
2	apple liqueur	40 ml (1½ oz)
3	lemon juice, freshly squeezed	30 ml (1 oz)
4	cloudy apple juice	15 ml (½ oz)
5	ginger bitters	2 dashes

EQUIPMENT

Shaker, strainer

METHOD

Shake the vodka, apple liqueur, lemon and apple juices vigorously over ice. Strain into a martini glass or coupe and top with a couple of dashes of ginger bitters.

GLASS TYPE: MARTINI
OR COUPE

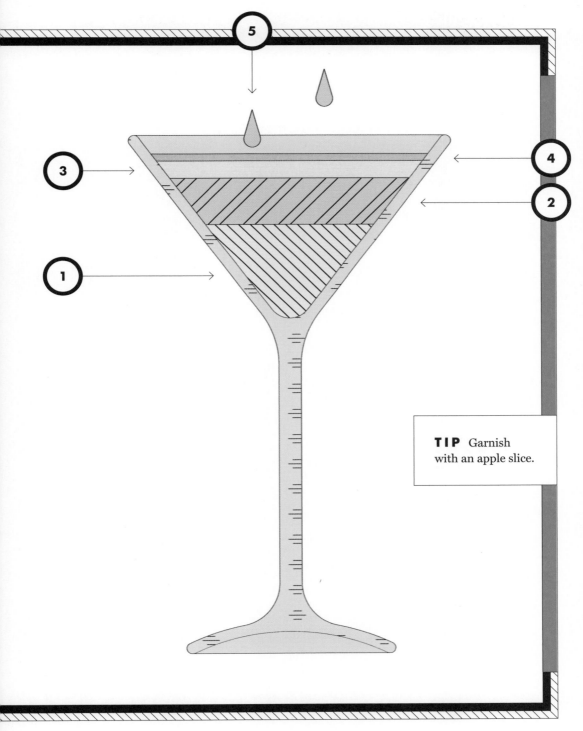

TIP Garnish with an apple slice.

SUNBURN

This ruby-toned cocktail has a dry, rather grown-up edge, powered by cranberry and blood orange juice and smoothed out with buttery gold tequila. This works perfectly as a solo drink.

INGREDIENTS

1	gold tequila		37.5 ml (1¼ oz)
2	orange liqueur		15 ml (½ oz)
3	blood orange juice, freshly squeezed		60 ml (2 oz)
4	cranberry juice		60 ml (2 oz)
5	blood orange slices		to garnish

EQUIPMENT

Bar spoon

METHOD

Pour all of the ingredients (except the garnish) into a highball filled with ice. Stir well and add the blood orange slices to garnish.

GLASS TYPE:
HIGHBALL

TIP Makes a great BBQ punch.

PINE FOREST

Pine tips – the sweet, aromatic and bright green new needles at the end of fir twigs – make a delicious homemade syrup. Mix with gin and chilled nutty almond milk and you have yourself a delicious, sweet-smelling cocktail.

INGREDIENTS

1	gin	60 ml (2 oz)
2	almond milk	60 ml (2 oz)
3	Pine Tip Syrup (see flavoured syrup method, page 31)	30 ml (1 oz)
4	pine tips	to garnish

EQUIPMENT

Shaker

METHOD

Shake the liquids over ice, strain into a coupe and garnish with freshly picked pine tips.

GLASS TYPE:
COUPE

214

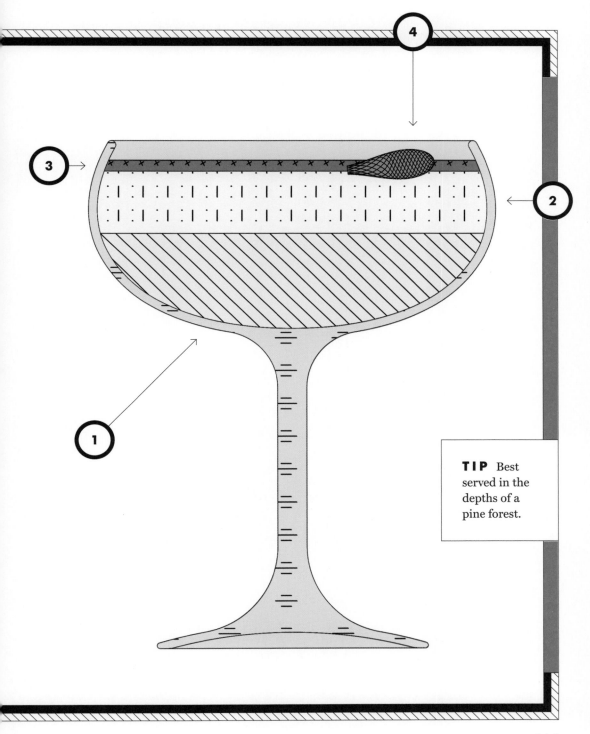

TIP Best served in the depths of a pine forest.

BRAMBLE

Imagine an autumnal English hedgerow liquidised into a glass. This fresh, berry-studded and herby cocktail is best served over crushed ice – or make it long with chilled soda water.

INGREDIENTS

1	blackberries	handful
2	gin	60 ml (2 oz)
3	lemon juice, freshly squeezed	15 ml (½ oz)
4	Simple Syrup (page 29)	splash
5	crème de mûre	splash
6	blackberries	to garnish
7	fresh mint sprig	to garnish

EQUIPMENT

Muddler

METHOD

Gently muddle the handful of fresh blackberries with gin, lemon juice and simple syrup. Add crushed ice and a generous splash of crème de mûre and garnish with fresh blackberries and mint.

GLASS TYPE:
TUMBLER
OR HIGHBALL

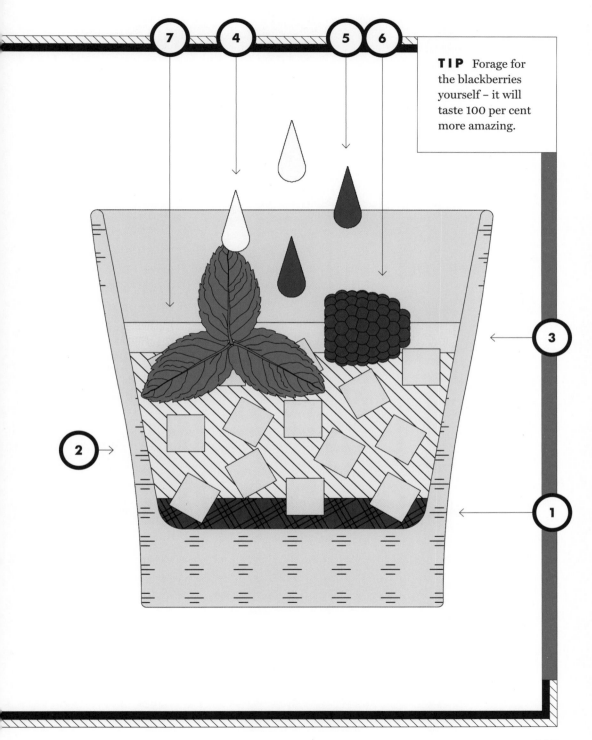

SHERBET SNOW

Old Persian kings would drink their sherbet – a luxurious sweetened fruit juice – cooled with mountain snow. This contemporary version is a little more trustworthy (yellow snow, anyone?): it's tart with lime, sweetened with honey and magically aromatic with a touch of orange blossom.

INGREDIENTS

1	white rum	60 ml (2 oz)
2	Cointreau	15 ml (½ oz)
3	lime juice, freshly squeezed	15 ml (½ oz)
4	lemon sorbet	120 ml (4 oz)
5	orange blossom water	2 dashes
6	honey, with a splash of hot water	15 ml (½ oz)
7	lime zest, finely grated	to garnish

EQUIPMENT

Shaker

METHOD

Shake the liquids and sorbet over ice and pour into a chilled coupe. Stir the hot water into the honey to help dilute, then drizzle over the top. Add lime zest to garnish.

GLASS TYPE:
COUPE

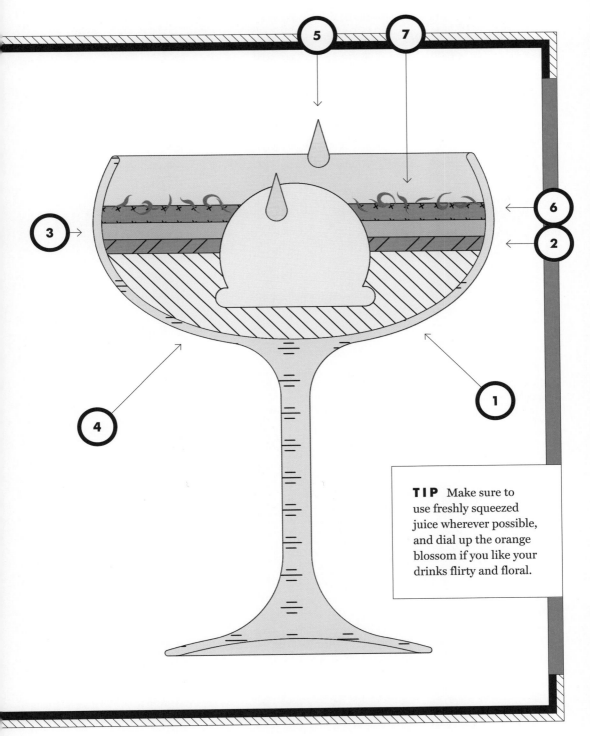

TIP Make sure to use freshly squeezed juice wherever possible, and dial up the orange blossom if you like your drinks flirty and floral.

THE RUDOLPH

Gin, elderflower liqueur and chilled Champagne: a perfect festive season cocktail with a string of Rudolph noses for added schmaltz. Looks great in a martini glass, coupe or Champagne flute.

INGREDIENTS

1	gin	60 ml (2 oz)
2	St-Germain elderflower liqueur	30 ml (1 oz)
3	chilled Champagne	to top up
4	string of redcurrants	to garnish

METHOD

Pour the gin and elderflower liqueur into a chilled glass, top with Champagne and garnish with a string of redcurrants.

GLASS TYPE:
COUPE
OR MARTINI

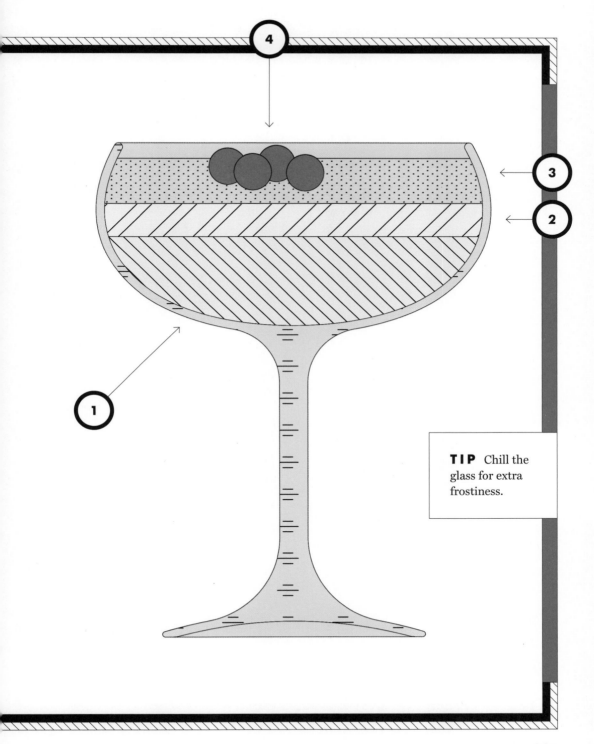

TIP Chill the glass for extra frostiness.

After Dinner, Early Hours

After dinner digestifs or eye-crossingly powerful late-night pick-me-ups. No room for dessert? Mix up an Ultimate Espresso Martini, Grasshopper or Almond White Russian. Sweet AF.

ULTIMATE ESPRESSO MARTINI

This luxury version of the posh party classic uses Patrón's delicious XO Cafe tequila-based liqueur in place of Kahlúa and chocolate bitters for a mind-blowing aroma.

INGREDIENTS

1	premium vodka	60 ml (2 oz)
2	Patrón XO Cafe liqueur	50 ml (1¾ oz)
3	chilled espresso	50 ml (1¾ oz)
4	chocolate bitters	3 dashes

EQUIPMENT

Shaker, strainer

METHOD

Shake the vodka, Patrón and espresso over ice, strain into a chilled glass and top with chocolate bitters.

GLASS TYPE: MARTINI OR COUPE

TIP For the perfect after-dinner sipper serve in a tumbler over ice.

GRASSHOPPER

The classic mint-chocolate cream dessert drink favoured by Halloween party guests and drag queens (after the Daiquiris are drunk dry). The originator of this delicious Muppet-green cocktail is thought to be Philip Guichet of Tujague's bar in New Orleans in 1918. We salute you, sir.

INGREDIENTS

1	vodka	25 ml (¾ oz)
2	cream	25 ml (¾ oz)
3	crème de menthe	15 ml (½ oz)
4	white crème de cacao	15 ml (½ oz)
5	grated chocolate	to garnish

EQUIPMENT

Shaker, strainer

METHOD

Shake the liquids over ice and strain into a martini glass or coupe. Garnish with a little grated chocolate.

GLASS TYPE:
MARTINI OR COUPE

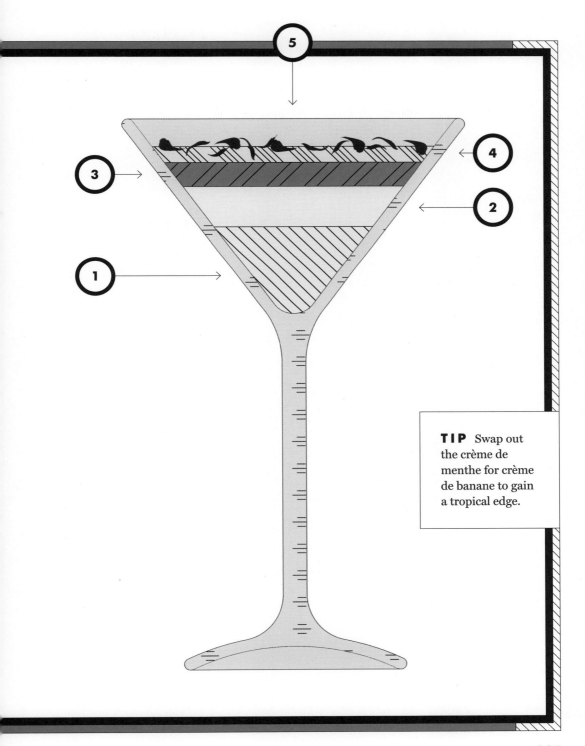

TIP Swap out the crème de menthe for crème de banane to gain a tropical edge.

ESPRESSO OLD FASHIONED

The annoyingly refined, grown up big brother to the Espresso Martini, this fresh AF Espresso Old Fashioned is as powerful as it is simple. Just-made espresso from your local café raises this tasty pick me up to dizzying heights, but a good-quality home-brew would also do the trick. Rye gives a little fiery kick, and a demerara-like, soft bourbon or blended whisky works perfectly.

INGREDIENTS

1	fresh espresso (about a double shot), room temperature	60 ml (2 oz)
2	bourbon or rye	30 ml (1 oz)
3	Simple Syrup (page 29)	10 ml (⅓ oz)
4	Peychaud's bitters	dash
5	lemon twist	to garnish

EQUIPMENT

Mixing glass, bar spoon, strainer

METHOD

Add the liquids to a mixing glass and stir over ice until frosty. Strain into a tumbler over ice, lemon twist over drink, then discard.

GLASS TYPE:
HEAVY TUMBLER

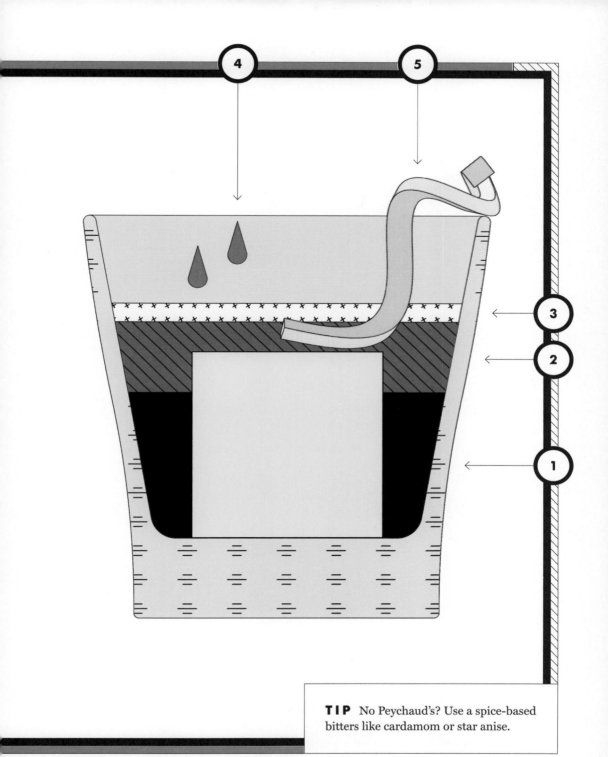

TIP No Peychaud's? Use a spice-based bitters like cardamom or star anise.

LICK DRINK BITE

One of the most prolific ways to drink tequila, yet the one that most people seem to get back to front. Lick the salt, drink the tequila, bite the fruit. Freeze the tequila first for an icy, less powerful-tasting shot.

INGREDIENTS

1	gold tequila	30 ml (1 oz)
2	sea salt	large pinch
3	lime or blood orange wedge	1 per shot

METHOD

Pour one shot of tequila into a shot glass. Put a little sea salt on the back of your hand. First lick the salt, then shoot the tequila. Finally, suck the lime.

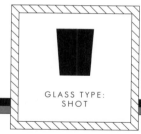

GLASS TYPE:
SHOT

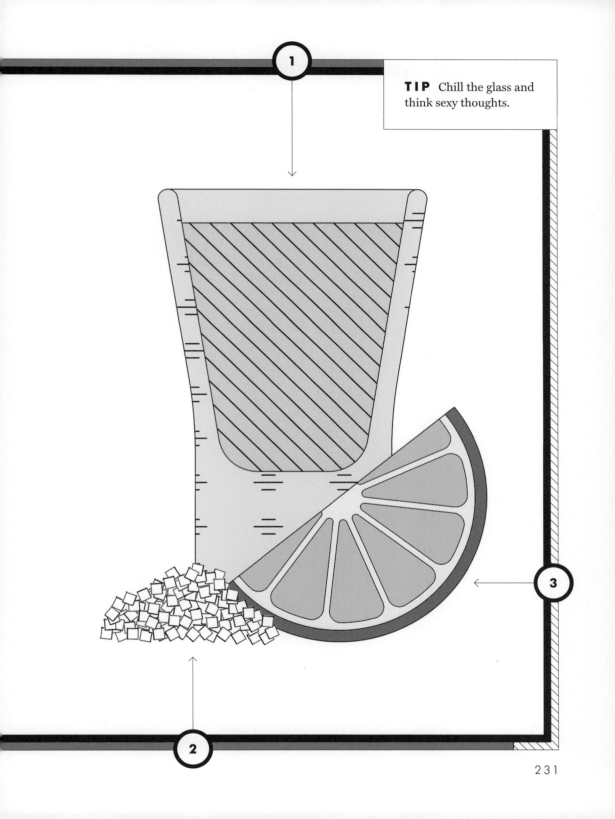

TIP Chill the glass and think sexy thoughts.

ALMOND WHITE RUSSIAN

This rather attractive, almond-edged White Russian swaps out fresh cream for delicious nut milk and is all the better for it. Make sure your vodka is super-chilled in the freezer and use almond milk straight from the refrigerator. Serve as a dessert – or instead of your morning latte, because why not?

INGREDIENTS

1	super-chilled vanilla vodka	30 ml (1 oz)
2	Kahlúa coffee liqueur	30 ml (1 oz)
3	chilled almond milk	125 ml (4 oz)

METHOD

Add the vodka and Kahlúa to a tumbler with a single large ice cube and gently pour over the almond milk to create an ombré effect.

GLASS TYPE:
TUMBLER

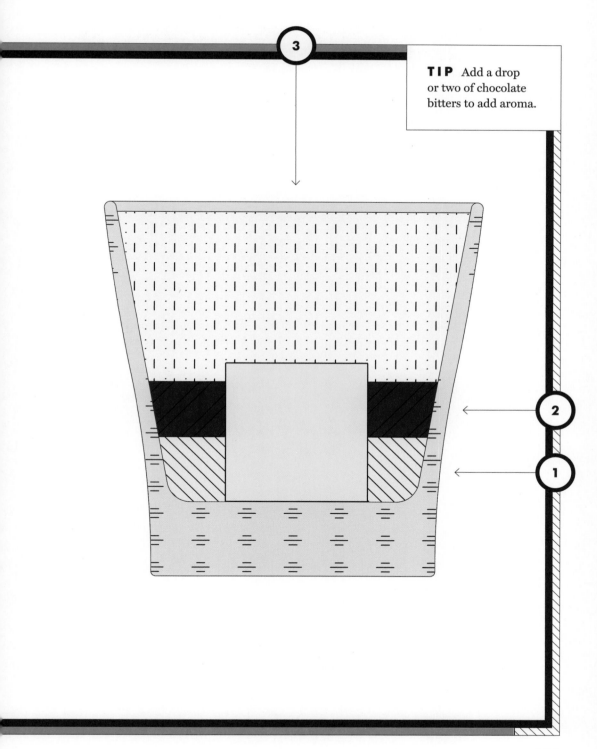

3

TIP Add a drop or two of chocolate bitters to add aroma.

FROZEN COSMO

Some call the Frozen Cosmo a textural reworking of the classic cranberry cocktail, others call it the gal pal's slushie, but it's delicious whatever you call it. Use a tough-ass blender and crushed (not cubed) ice for a truly silky drink.

INGREDIENTS

1	Absolut Citron vodka	45 ml (1½ oz)
2	Cointreau	15 ml (½ oz)
3	cranberry juice	30 ml (1 oz)
4	lime juice, freshly squeezed	15 ml (½ oz)
5	lime wheels	to garnish

EQUIPMENT

Blender

METHOD

Add the liquids to a high-power blender with crushed ice and whizz until slushie-like. Pour into a glass and top with a splash more cranberry to loosen, if needed. Garnish with lime wheels.

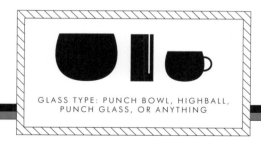

GLASS TYPE: PUNCH BOWL, HIGHBALL, PUNCH GLASS, OR ANYTHING

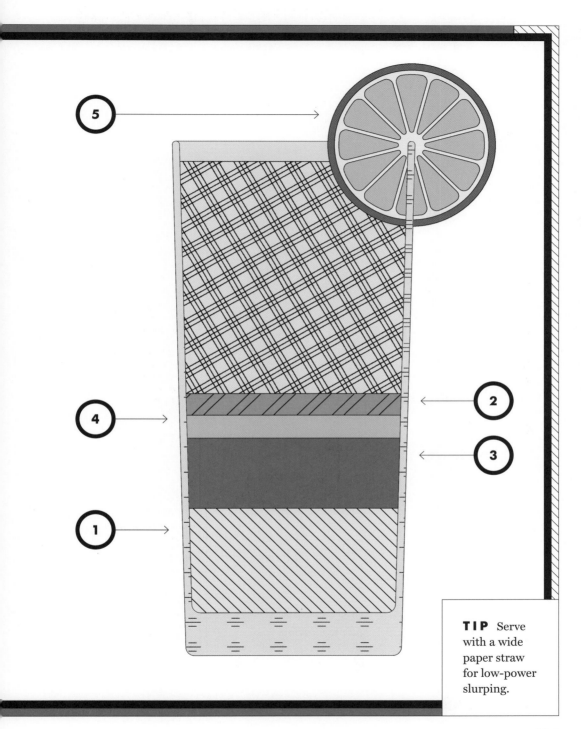

TIP Serve with a wide paper straw for low-power slurping.

ESPRESSO MARTINI

AKA gal's rocket fuel. This classic cocktail is the night-time pick-me-up for those who claim they have pilates in the morning and need to retire early. Serve them an Espresso Martini after dinner and watch them tap dance on your coffee table until the early hours.

INGREDIENTS

1	premium vodka	60 ml (2 oz)
2	Kahlúa coffee liqueur	50 ml (1¾ oz)
3	chilled espresso	50 ml (1¾ oz)
4	coffee beans	to garnish

EQUIPMENT

Shaker, strainer

METHOD

Shake the liquids over ice and strain into a chilled martini glass or coupe. Garnish with 2–3 coffee beans.

GLASS TYPE:
MARTINI OR COUPE

TIP No coffee beans? Grated chocolate will do nicely.

FRENCH MARTINI

The silky, sweet and berry-infused French Martini is a classic. Use Chambord for an authentic taste, fresh or premium pineapple juice, and shake well to create a plump foam top. Swap out the premium vodka for vanilla vodka for extra Frenchiness.

INGREDIENTS

1	premium vodka	30 ml (1 oz)
2	Chambord	30 ml (1 oz)
3	pineapple juice	30 ml (1 oz)

EQUIPMENT

Shaker, strainer

METHOD

Shake all the ingredients vigorously over ice and strain into a glass.

GLASS TYPE:
MARTINI OR COUPE

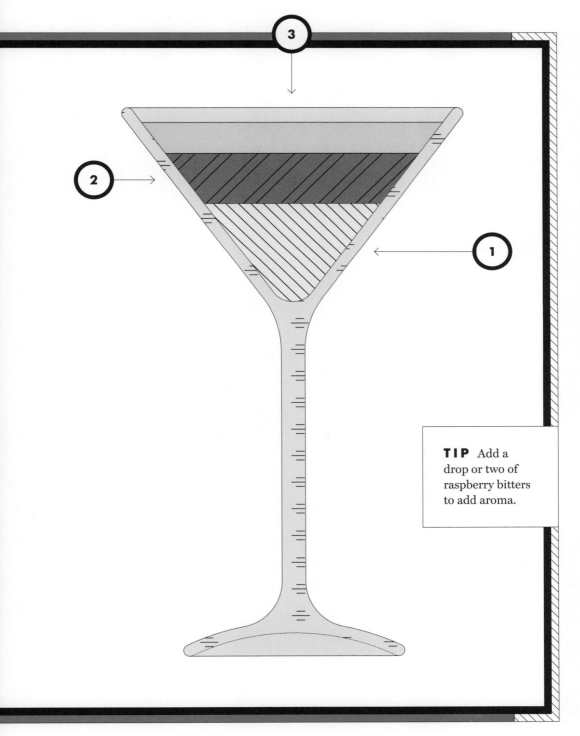

TIP Add a drop or two of raspberry bitters to add aroma.

Hot Toddies & Tongue Burners

Turn up the heat: from a fragrant, frangipane-like winter drink to rival mulled wine, to a buttery classic, booze powers these uplifting drinks. Is it getting hot in here?

HOT SPICED PEAR & GINGER

Many of us consume at least eight pints too many of mulled wine each Christmas. This spiced pear, ginger and apple concoction is a perfect and rather classy upgrade.

INGREDIENTS (SERVES 10)

1	Stone's Ginger Wine	250 ml (8½ oz)
2	cloudy apple juice	1.5 litres (2½ pints)
3	lime juice, freshly squeezed	250 ml (8½ oz)
4	ripe pears, sliced	1–2
5	fresh ginger, sliced	1 thumb-sized piece
6	cardamom pods, bashed open	4
7	star anise, bashed	1
8	cinnamon sticks	2
9	demerara sugar	2 tbsp
10	spiced rum	250 ml (8½ oz)

EQUIPMENT

Pan, ladle

METHOD

Bring the ingredients (apart from the rum) to a boil and gently simmer until the sugar has dissolved. Add 25 ml (1 oz) rum to each glass or mug, ladle over the hot apple juice and pears and serve.

GLASS TYPE:
HEATPROOF GLASS
OR MUG

242

TIP Leave out the ginger wine if you fancy your Christmas drinks a little less alcoholic.

243

HOT-BUTTERED RUM

A cold-weather classic, this hot-buttered rum will warm you up in cracks and crevices you didn't know you had. Straining the liquid helps distribute the butter and remove the lumpy solids, and cardamom bitters add an intoxicating fragrance. It's time to butter up.

INGREDIENTS

1	demerara sugar	2 tsp
2	unsalted butter	2 tsp
3	cardamom bitters	dash
4	ground cinnamon	pinch
5	freshly grated nutmeg	pinch
6	cloves	3
7	spiced rum	60 ml (2 oz)
8	freshly grated nutmeg	to garnish

EQUIPMENT

Milk pan, fine mesh sieve

METHOD

Add the ingredients (apart from the rum) to a small milk pan over a low heat, stirring until the butter and sugar have melted into a syrup. Remove from the heat, stir in the rum and strain through a fine mesh sieve. Serve dusted with nutmeg in a heatproof glass.

GLASS TYPE:
HEATPROOF GLASS
WITH HANDLE

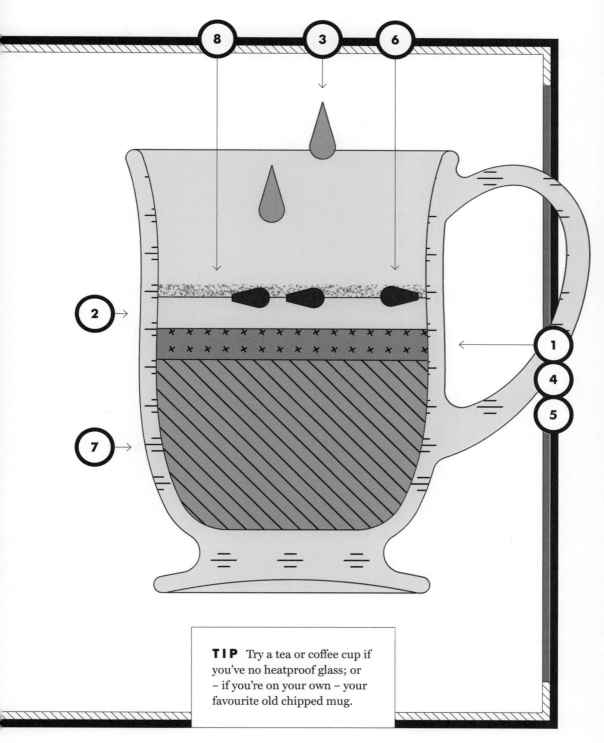

TIP Try a tea or coffee cup if you've no heatproof glass; or – if you're on your own – your favourite old chipped mug.

MEXICAN HOT CHOCOLATE

This spiked hot chocolate is sweet and rich with a subtle chilli heat and eye-crossingly intoxicating aroma. Cardamom is, of course, not particularly Mexican, but it's a delicious addition.

INGREDIENTS

1	milk	200–250 ml (7–9 oz)
2	dark chocolate	3 squares
3	cocoa powder	1 tbsp
4	brown sugar	1 tsp
5	cardamom pod, bashed open	1
6	cayenne powder	pinch
7	mezcal	60 ml (2 oz)
8	whipped cream	to garnish
9	grated chocolate	to garnish

EQUIPMENT

Saucepan

METHOD

Warm the milk in a saucepan and add the chocolate, cocoa powder, sugar, cardamom pod and cayenne. Heat gently until all the ingredients have combined. Pour the mezcal into a mug and add the warm chocolate mixture. Top with whipped cream and grated chocolate (and a little extra cayenne if you wish).

GLASS TYPE:
HEATPROOF MUG

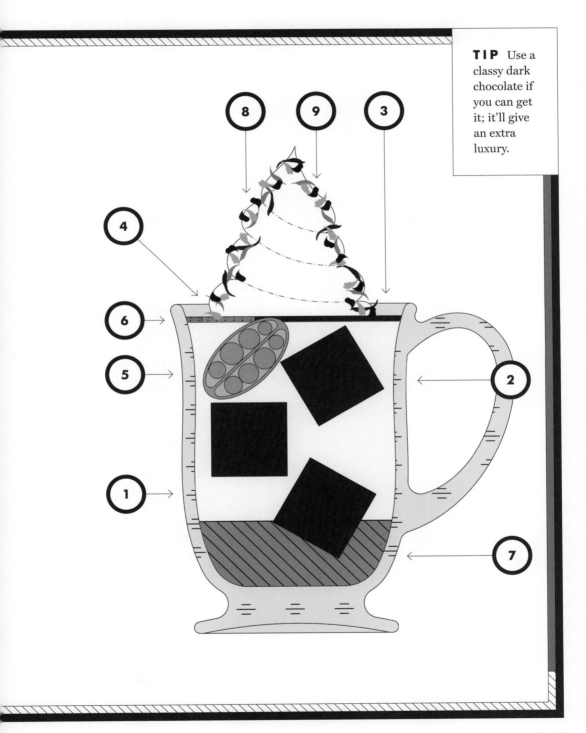

TIP Use a classy dark chocolate if you can get it; it'll give an extra luxury.

247

HOT RUM TODDY

The kind of drink your grandpa makes you when you're sick as a child – but then your grandma catches him and bats it out of your hand. The mysterious cure-all properties of hot alcohol are perhaps a disputed fact, but it certainly tastes good. In the words of everyone's grandpa, 'This'll put hairs on your chest!'

INGREDIENTS

1	spiced rum	90 ml (3 oz)
2	runny honey	4 tbsp
3	lemon juice, freshly squeezed	15 ml (½ oz)
4	orange twist	1 large
5	cardamom bitters	dash
6	freshly grated nutmeg	to garnish
7	cinnamon stick	to garnish

EQUIPMENT

Bar spoon

METHOD

Add the rum, honey, lemon juice, orange twist, bitters and nutmeg to a heatproof glass. Top up with boiling water and stir until the honey dissolves. Add a cinnamon stick and serve.

GLASS TYPE:
HEATPROOF GLASS
MUG

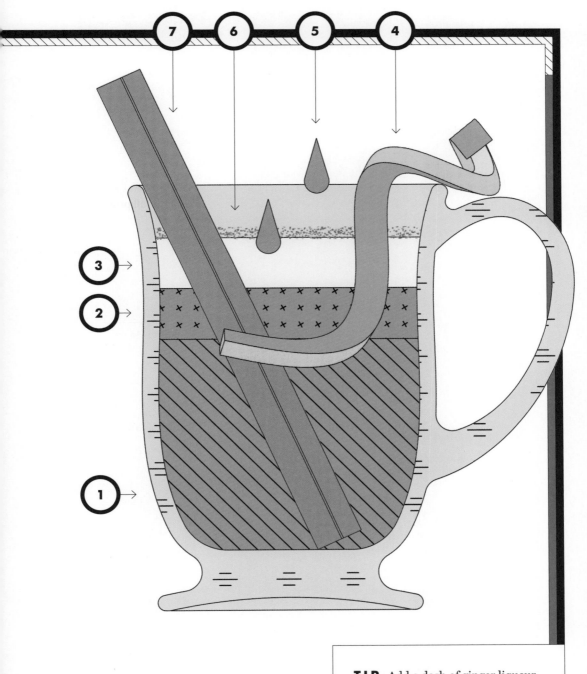

TIP Add a dash of ginger liqueur if you're feeling particularly peaky.

DICKENS' HOT GIN PUNCH

It's not all about summer-quenching and dithering about with a cucumber: hot gin punch is the perfect winter warmer with a rich literary history. Here follows a recipe close to the gin punch that Charles Dickens' Mr Micawber gets tipsy on in.

INGREDIENTS (SERVES 10–12)

1	premium gin	750 ml (24 fl oz/3 cups)
2	Madeira wine	750 ml (24 fl oz/3 cups)
3	whole cloves	pinch
4	ground nutmeg	pinch
5	cinnamon powder	generous pinch
6	Spiced Brown Sugar Syrup (see flavoured syrup method, page 31)	dash
7	lemon juice, freshly squeezed	90 ml (3 oz)
8	lemon slices	to garnish
9	pineapple chunks	1 small pineapple
10	honey	4 tablespoons

EQUIPMENT

Heavy-based saucepan

METHOD

Add all the ingredients to a heavy-based saucepan and gently heat for around 30 minutes to let the flavours infuse, adding a more honey or lemon to taste. The flavour intensifies the longer you it simmer. Ladle into punch glasses – or pour it from a teapot if you're that way inclined.

GLASS TYPE:
HEATPROOF
PUNCH GLASSES

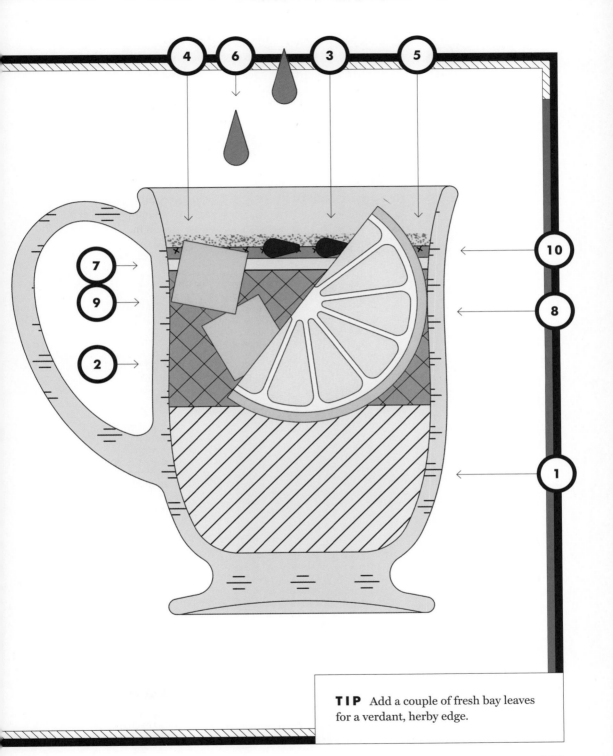

TIP Add a couple of fresh bay leaves for a verdant, herby edge.

INDEX

ABOUT
DAN JONES

Dan Jones is a London-based writer reporting on cocktails, style, grooming and queer culture. A self-described drinking enthusiast, he is best-selling author of books about booze – including the best-selling *Gin: Shake, Muddle, Stir* – and a very messy home-mixer. His favourite drink is a Dirty Martini, extra filthy.